Praise for *Leadership in 100 Days*

"Very pragmatic self-study guide that with personal discipline provides a clear road map towards (increased) success."
—Hans Toggweiler, CEO Americas, DHL

"This is being seen by the senior leadership as having the potential to shape all of how Johnson & Johnson does business."
—Sandra Thompson, Vice President Human Resources, Animas, a Johnson & Johnson Company

"*Leadership in 100 Days* combines the best of Thomas D. Zweifel's books. It's witty and fun to read, full of fascinating stories, and eminently practical. And it delivers what most leadership books don't: It gives you real access to leadership, day after day, brick by brick, on the job of making something happen. For any executive who needs to reboot his or her leadership, and for companies that need better leaders."
—Hanspeter Mathis, Managing Director, Uvex Safety Switzerland

"Incredibly useful... The Global Leader Pyramid® mak
simple to integrate into one's life the system of hum
communication that has changed the world. Wh
conscious of how you communicate, and car
communication to your specific ends, yo
ideas with the power of all who you com
the GLP to gain clarity in the dynamics of c
Think first, find where you are in the Pyrami ve your
meetings, conversations and relationships to ac and
success!"
—Judd Maltin, Systems Principal Engineer, Dell

"Just today was again a moment in which the Global Leader Pyramid® helped me to solve a problem I had grappled with

for a long time. The Pyramid gave me the breakthrough idea. Suddenly everything ran completely by itself. Actually it would be very easy to prevent this type of problem by proceeding consistently according to the Global Leader Pyramid®."
—Frederic Mueller, General Manager, Insulation & Components, ABB

"As complexity grows, emotional intelligence and inherent leadership skills are more important than ever. *Leadership in 100 Days* definitely stimulated my daily self-coaching efforts for improvement in this domain through a pragmatic and illustrative context. The book animates and helps to carry out personal assignments on a day-to-day basis. I will warmly recommend it to my leadership team."
—Dr. Felix Obrist, CEO, Nahrin AG

"When you find yourself more than ten years later applying the tools you've learned, still recognizing their power and feeling the gratitude that these tools or methods are now part of you—always there to help you move forward and thrive... then you know that whoever brought them to you is nothing short of brilliant. Thomas was one of such rare people, and if I were to name the three greatest methods/concepts I've learned from him, it would be: the Global Leader Pyramid®; declaring a breakdown; and the power of making clear, whole-hearted and simple declarations when conversations get foggy. Thank you, Thomas!"
—Eva Steinhaus, Director, Commerzbank AG

"Thanks to his concept in 5 levels and its practical implementation for 100 days, Thomas D. Zweifel's book helps us to analyze how we manage ourselves, our companies, our employees and our customers in order to achieve our defined goals. It gives us excellent recipes in order to become a good leader. The combination of theoretical and practical exercises is particularly powerful. I would highly recommend this book not only to newcomers in management but also to people who

already have a great deal of experience."
—Bernard Frossard, CEO, Connectis

"A fast, simple and effective tool."
—Leander Isler, Board of Directors, Gessner AG

"*Leadership in 100 Days* is a pressure-cooker of a book, with a force that propels you forward day after day as you build your leadership—all the while getting to what you really want. Although you cannot replace real-time conversations with a live coach, this is indeed a 'coach in a book' that confronts you with your own blind-spots and charts a course you might not take on your own—the path of leadership. A huge return on investment."
—Martin Naville, CEO, Swiss-American Chamber of Commerce

"*Leadership in 100 Days* is really a complete methodology that day after day developed my leadership and pushed me to action. During my catalytic project, I could experiment with theories and tools that I integrated into all my projects. Thank you for giving me the opportunity to experience this adventure!"
—Frédéric Cina, Production Manager & Food Technologist

"We make decisions abiding by sub-conscious dictums and internal thinking processes of which we are unaware. *Leadership in 100 Days* holds these processes up to the mirror, enabling us to be cognizant of our the method and our madness, and injecting the flexibility to abandon dogma and pivot towards new more effective strategies and decisions."
—Lawrence Obstfeld, CEO, Image Navigation

"The book *Leadership in 100 Days* will always be with me in my future professional career."
—Pierre Füllemann, Head of Network Engineering, Skyguide

"I will definitely recommend the *Leadership in 100 Days* book to my people."
—Markus Hostettler, Leiter Risikomanagement und Risikocontrolling, BKW Energie AG

"I recommend *Leadership in 100 Days*. This book is very pragmatic and offers a different and very powerful vision of leadership."
—Frédéric Duruz, Responsable de Filiale, PostFinance

"I wish I had had Zweifel's tools 35 years ago when I was starting out."
—Werner Brandmayr, President, ConocoPhillips-Europe

Dr. Thomas D. Zweifel

Leadership in 100 Days

This edition published by iHorizon
For information address iHorizon, New York, NY 10003.

ISBN 978-1-09166-743-3

Library of Congress Cataloging-in-Publication Data

Zweifel, Thomas D., 1962-
Leadership in 100 days : your systematic self-coaching roadmap to power and impact—and your future / Dr. Thomas D. Zweifel
2nd ed.
Includes bibliographical references and notes.
ISBN 978-1-09166-743-3 (hbk. : alk. Paper)
1. Leadership. 2. Leadership—Management.

Manufactured in the United States of America.

Leadership in 100 Days

Your Systematic Self-Coaching Roadmap to Power and Impact—and Your Future

2nd Revised Edition

Dr. Thomas D. Zweifel

iHorizon

Table of Contents

Dr. Thomas D. Zweifel

Preface

I have no theory.
I only show something.
I show reality...
I take those who listen to me by the hand
and lead them to the window.
I push open the window and point outside. –
I have no theory, but I lead a conversation.
Martin Buber

We face a VUCA world – a world of volatility, uncertainty, complexity and ambiguity. Whether it's the threat of terrorism or the possibility of a global economic meltdown; whether it's migration pressures or environmental destruction; whether it's white-collar crime or institutional corruption; or whether it's the breakdown of trust in governments, the church or the media – what is the lynchpin issue that underlies all others?

Leadership in 100 Days asserts (and we concur) that the root cause is the lack of twenty-first century leadership – leadership ready to meet today's unprecedented challenges.

Of times like these the late economist and philosopher Kenneth Boulding said, "The greatest need for leadership is in the dark. It is when the system is changing so rapidly ... that old prescriptions and old wisdoms can only lead to catastrophe and leadership is necessary to call people to the very strangeness of the new world being born."

The old leadership model is bankrupt. Why? Because a new leadership landscape – globalization and democratization, flattening organizational hierarchies and virtual teams, outsourcing and offshoring, the Internet and Blockchain, social networks and ubiquitous media – makes leading a more complex challenge than ever.

Even the twentieth century's greatest leaders might have had a hard time leading in the twenty-first. President Franklin D. Roosevelt's debilitating polio would be all over the Internet. John F. Kennedy's chronic extramarital trysts would haunt him while he faced not one but multiple enemies. And Winston Churchill would be on YouTube for his "battle with the bottle."

Churchill was famous for saying that the higher you rise, the more clearly you see the big picture of vision and strategy. (He also said, presciently, that the higher the ape climbs, the more you can see of his bottom.) But is that still true today, when the receptionist or the front-line salesperson interface with customers every day and may have as much insight into the market as top managers and board members? Even the military recognizes that soldiers on the ground in Sadr City or Seoul may have more access to local strategic intelligence than Pentagon planners or commanders at headquarters, and need to take part in strategic decision-making. In complex environments, top-down leadership no longer works.

The good news is that leadership is no longer confined to the realm of the select few. Throughout history, leadership was scarce. Now it is a public good. Google and Wikipedia put knowledge at people's fingertips with the click of a mouse. Skype and Facebook connect them across the world for free or next to nothing. In the last century, consumers chose among a few TV channels and magazines; by 2007 there were 70 million blogs on the World Wide Web. MySpace and YouTube, where 65,000 videos are posted daily, democratize entertainment and give anyone a shot at being a musician or movie director.

Thanks to Macs and Web 2.0, you too can be an industrial designer in the new "design democracy." So-called "lead users" are often on the forefront of innovation and product development, from software to high-performance windsurfing equipment. Patients have stopped blindly trusting their doctors and instead demand answers and choice—something unthinkable a generation ago, when doctors were thought to be omniscient demigods whose judgment no-one dared question.

But how are we to lead in this new environment? It's a tough question. Take a cue from Warren Buffett. When the chairman of Berkshire Hathaway, one financial services company to emerge from the crisis unscathed, announced his plans to hire a younger person (or several) to understudy him in managing Berkshire's investments, he did *not* mention financial savvy or technical skills or even strategic planning. Qualified candidates, Buffett noted, must possess "independent thinking, emotional stability, and a keen understanding of both human and institutional behavior."

Thomas D. Zweifel, the author of this seminal WorkBook, calls it "The 3 Cs": *Co-leadership* (not leading top-down or imposing solutions unilaterally, but empowering leaders at all levels to own the strategy and make decisions); *Communication* (not only broadcasting down the hierarchy, but listening up to get vital intelligence from the market and the field into the boardroom and into the strategy); and *Cross-cultural* savvy (working with people of other value-systems, standing in their shoes and seeing the world from their point of view to foresee strategic moves by adversaries and competitors).

A generation ago, leaders could get away without the 3 Cs. Churchill could lead top-down (when reminded that leaders should keep their ear to the ground, he quipped, "If I do that, I shall be detected in a somewhat ungainly position"). He could give brilliant speeches but did not have to listen. And he could insult Mahatma Gandhi as "that little naked man." Today that is no longer possible.

Leadership in 100 Days gives you the tools to lead successfully in the 21st century.

> As Herb Kelleher, the former leader of Southwest Airlines, the rare airline that has remained consistently profitable, put it, "a humanistic approach to business *can* pay dividends—and believe me, I'm *not* off my meds!"

If more leaders had followed Buffett's and Kelleher's example, they would not be in the predicament they are in. Neither would we.

Prof. Eric Décosterd
Director
Executive MBA
HEG Fribourg
Switzerland

Prof. Jaime Alonso
Dean, EGADE
TEC Monterrey
Mexico City Campus
Mexico

Prof. Thierry Grange
President
Ecole de
Management
Grenoble
France

How to Use this WorkBook

What you are holding in your hands (or staring at on your screen) is much more than a book. *Leadership in 100 Days* is a roadmap to your future as a leader. Whatever goal you put your mind to, the tools in these pages will give you the capacity to achieve it.

Of course there is never a guarantee in life. "Life is," John Lennon quipped famously, "what happens when you had other plans." But thousands of my clients and students (3,258 and counting, to be Swiss and precise about it)—not to mention myself—have utilized these tools to meet strategic imperatives, in business and in life, over and over again, for more than three decades.

I have used this system to achieve pretty much everything I have achieved, including building a successful company and selling it, publishing seven books, teaching at Columbia, and securing my financial freedom, to name but a few examples.

Others have used this WorkBook to catalyze the achievement of their own dreams, from launching a Brazilian restaurant in Harlem to taking their family company into eCommerce, from boosting innovation in their firm to building a prototype and bringing a new product to market, from landing their dream job to creating a NGO in Benin, from creating a Blockchain startup to bringing the Olympic Games to Jerusalem. (Well, this last one is still underway, and frankly it's a bit of a long shot.)

Teams have profited from the system to reduce the overtime (and budget creep) for a satellite build from 100% overtime (and over budget) to 10%; to kill the billing backlog in a law-firm; to grow retail sales by 11% while retail in the industry declined; or to save $200 million by offshoring 5,000 knowledge workers while maintaining morale in the company.

One student used the roadmap to build an executive jet company. A few years later he called me to report that his company was now on *Inc.* magazine's list of the 500 fastest-growing companies. (Today I am honored to sit on the board of the company.)

The purpose of this WorkBook is to give both experienced and emerging leaders a vehicle (that's the original meaning of the word "coach" anyway; before there were automobiles, horse-drawn coaches brought people to their desired destinations) for self-paced, systematic self-coaching. In other words, the WorkBook is a guide and pathway for jumpstarting your own vision and achieving what you want to achieve.

The WorkBook is designed to serve as a companion to managers or would-be leaders at all levels in your company, or for students of leadership, management or public administration in a university or technical school.

Learning leadership is not easy, but the procedure is simple. Ideally first thing each morning, before you face the onslaught of the day, read the module for that day so that its themes can permeate your day. Every day's module starts with a short quote that aims to give you an inspiring context and food for thought for that day. The reading should take you about five minutes.

After studying a day's module, you ideally carry out the assignment for that day immediately. If you cannot, schedule yourself for a specific time that day when you *will* do the assignment, no kidding—and no matter what other pressing demands may come up during that time.

Make sure you don't fall behind. Remember that Michael Jordan became a basketball virtuoso through his willingness to do "the extra shots at night" when nobody was watching. Jordan did not have the expectation that he would become a champion simply by virtue of some innate talent or by playing it by ear. He knew that he needed to develop his championship through a daily drill. The tennis crack Roger Federer (who like me hails from the Swiss city of Basel) built his greatness over 800 matches and tens of thousands of practice sessions. It's the same in any field of human endeavor, whether you want to become a great pianist or doctor or leader: you develop excellence and greatness through daily practice, day in, day out.

You do this for nobody other than yourself. The world does not necessarily call for your leadership, so it's your choice whether you want to go for leadership or not.

Such daily practice should not be too difficult, since you will have the opportunity to design, launch, and implement a 100-Day Catalytic Project (Day 2) that jumpstarts your own 5-year vision (Day 27). The notion of the Catalytic Project comes from a famous quote by Mahatma Gandhi: "Be today the future that you wish for the world." You do the Catalytic Project as a pilot, a proof-of-concept, a laboratory in which you can test your leadership approach in the action of producing results. And these results, and your activities to cause them, should not be divorced from your day-to-day management but integrated with your objectives and daily work.

To your success. Have fun with the journey!

Day 1: What Is Leadership?

Date:_______

In the world to come, I shall not be asked,
"Why were you not Abraham?"
I shall be asked,
"Why were you not Zusya?"
Rabbi Zusya

Be warned now: Leadership is not neat, and it's not something you can simply tick off on a checklist. It is a messy affair, highly uncomfortable, often chaotic, especially when you deal with making and managing change. I don't recommend being a leader—unless of course you go with Theodore Roosevelt, who said:

> It is not the critic who counts: not the man who points out how the strong man stumbles or where the doer of deeds could have done better. The credit belongs to the man who is actually in the arena, whose face is marred by dust and sweat and blood, who strives valiantly, who errs and comes up short again and again, because there is no effort without error or shortcoming, but who knows the great enthusiasms, the great devotions, who spends himself for a worthy cause; who, at the best, knows, in the end, the triumph of high achievement, and who, at the worst, if he fails, at least he fails while daring greatly, so that his place shall never be with those cold and timid souls who knew neither victory nor defeat.[1]

(A second warning, while we're at it: As you may have gathered by now, I love quotes and will quite probably inundate you with them. If you don't like quotes, I respect that; just ignore them.) But enough disclaimers; let's get down to business.

Assignment. Write down the 3 best leaders you know. They could be in any walk of life (business, government, military, nonprofit, religious leaders, or even in your family); they could be alive today or leaders in history.

1.

2.

3.

Now write down the 3 worst, most despicable, awful, disgusting leaders you know. Again, they could be in any walk of life (and heaven forbid, even in your family).

1.

2.

3.

Based on your list of best and worst leaders, what are your criteria? What are the characteristics that great leaders possess and that bad leaders don't have, and vice versa?

How did you do? There are countless definitions of leadership, but such definitions are of limited utility. This module was designed for you to come up with your own criteria before you design and launch your own leadership challenge tomorrow. Leadership is an intensely individual endeavor that depends on your personal talents, situation, opportunities, and cultural background. For example, when I facilitate leadership workshops, most participants come up with Hitler as an example of a bad leader who led through intimidation and destruction; but in India, some people came up with Hitler as an example of great leadership. Why? Because from the vantage point of pre-independence India, he was seen as a liberator from the real enemy—the British empire.

Day 2: Your 100-Day Catalytic Project

Date:_______

We shall never learn what "is called" swimming, for example, or what it "calls for," by reading a treatise on swimming. Only the leap into the river tells us what is called swimming.
Martin Heidegger

You cannot learn swimming or painting by reading or knowing about swimming and painting. At some point you have to take action—by throwing yourself into the water or picking up a paintbrush. The same applies to learning the art and science of leadership: to become a leader, you have to throw yourself into the action of leading. The 100-Day Catalytic Project is designed for you to do just that.

The 100-Day Catalytic Project will be a laboratory for testing and developing your leadership (and the theories and tools covered in this course) in the action of producing real-world changes and results—on the way to achieving your 5-year vision. It is important that you work on your project weekly, applying your understanding/learning of each module's content to your project.

Assignment. Ask yourself: What accomplishment, by the end of the 100 days, would constitute a breakthrough (an entrepreneurial leap, a jump in productivity, a new way of doing business or a jump in the quality of life) for your organization and/or your community?

There are no restrictions on what your 100-Day Catalytic Project is about (well, as long as you don't propose an illegal or sinister operation like robbing a bank or organizing an international prostitution network). But the project needs to fulfill certain requirements:

- It needs to be **visionary**, i.e. correlated to your own vision of yourself as a leader five years from now, so that you live that future now (remember Gandhi's dictum: "Be today the future you wish for in the world").

- It needs to be **unpredictable,** i.e. not given by present or past circumstances but a breakthrough in both your results and your leadership capability—given by the future you are committed to.
- It needs to be **measurable,** i.e. you have to work from clear indicators of performance, and produce objectively measurable outcomes.
- It needs to be **inclusive,** i.e. include many other people, so that it "forces" you to be a leader with and for others.

Examples of Catalytic Projects leaders have undertaken:

- Bringing a new product to market in record time and producing $5 million revenue from this new product;
- Persuading the senior management team to adopt a new idea/vision/policy that was not in the cards;
- Producing a breakthrough result in sales;
- Building a new company and getting the first three clients or customers;
- Building a nongovernmental organization (NGO) and raising $25,000 for its work;
- Financing and opening a new restaurant, and hiring and training the staff;
- Persuading the governments of Israel and the Palestinian Authority to hold the Olympic Games in Jerusalem.

My 3-5 year vision this 100-Day Catalytic Project is designed to catalyze?

The current breakdown and/or opportunity my project will address?

My target audience?

My 100-Day Catalytic Project goals (measurable / specific / challenging / achievable / understandable / consistent with my organization's goals, mission, and principles) in the next 100 days?

The team members and background support (administrative, coaching) needed to make my project happen?

The milestones (monthly and weekly)?

My requests of others (specify who, what [actions/results], and by when)?

What could go wrong → what are key success factors?

How did you do? At a multinational energy company, Catalytic Projects focused on upgrading communications with gas station owners, and producing 1 Euro more per customer. → Result: the company produced 0.74 Euros more per customer (i.e. $74 million additional revenue). At a multinational pharma company, Catalytic Projects promoted collaboration between silos on bringing a product to market in Asia; changing the perception of the Australia subsidiary in the eyes of Swiss headquarters; and effective communication between silos. → Result: Within 9 months, the subsidiary was recognized by headquarters as a top performer. At a multinational bank, eight Catalytic Projects focused on facilitating a smooth transition to off-shoring 5,500 IT professionals. → Result: the bank ensured a smooth transition, reduced costs, and produced a breakthrough in annual net revenue.

Individual leaders have also undertaken Catalytic Projects like these: Reducing the overtime (and budget creep) for a satellite build from 100% overtime (and over budget) to 10%; entering a new strategic market like China and/or India; closing the backlog of unpaid invoices in a lawfirm; building a new consulting company and acquire the first paying client; building a Blockchain startup and bringing the product prototype to market; or revamping a team and producing a performance breakthrough in cost, speed and/or quality. The key is to go for catalyzing *your* vision.

Tip. To increase the probability of success, don't keep your 100-Day Catalytic Project a secret. Select a coaching partner: a colleague or friend who will hold you to your promises when you want to give up, and who will remember your commitments when you forget. Invite him/her to review your 100-Day Catalytic Project, create a working relationship with him/her, and schedule regular (at least weekly) check-in calls or meetings during the next 100 days.

Day 3: The Global Leader Pyramid®

Date:_______

If the only tool in one's possession is a hammer,
everything in sight begins to resemble a nail.
Abraham Kaplan

The Global Leader Pyramid® is based on constructivist philosophy. The basic idea is that reality is not fixed, but is the product of language. Leaders are defined as people who have conversations of value that empower others to achieve their goals. This theory puts leaders in charge and gives them tremendous power—regardless of their position, authority, or financial resources—simply by virtue of how they speak and listen.[2]

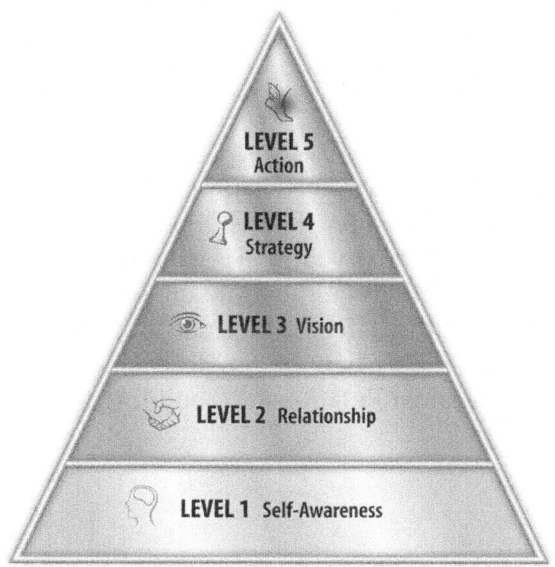

Figure 1: The Global Leader Pyramid®

Assignment. Draw the Global Leader Pyramid® (Self-Awareness, Relationship, Vision, Strategy, Action) below. Then map your three best and your three worst leaders (assignment from Day 1) along the Pyramid. At which level(s) of the Pyramid is/was each leader strong, and at which level(s) is/was each of them weak?

How did you do? To take our extreme example from Day 1, Hitler was effective at the Vision level (even though his vision was highly destructive), at Strategy, and at Action (albeit not for long); but he had zero Self-Awareness (no inkling of why he was so terribly angry at the defeat of Germany after World War I, or why he was so terribly bent on the destruction of world Jewry) and was weak at Relationship (building trust).

Day 4: Self-Assessment

Date:_______

One does not discover new lands
without consenting to lose sight
of the shore for a very long time.
André Gide

Assignment. Assess your leadership competencies (1=absent, 2=weak, 3=mediocre, 4=competent, 5=masterful). Be honest with yourself: neither too negative nor too boastful.

1. Self-Awareness

___ Checking your own assumptions, blind-spots, hidden motives, values; staying centered

___ Responsibility for the whole of your organization and mission

___ Beginner's mind; remaining a student; openness to coaching

2. Relationship / Communication

___ Specificity of speaking and listening; generating distinctions (e.g. in running meetings)

___ Ability to present information and/or your organization; persuade listeners

___ Listening for greatness, solutions, openings

___ Cultivating and deepening relationships

___ Enrollment: utilizing and integrating people's already-existing agenda

___ Facility with cultural diversity; standing in the shoes of the other person

___ Team skills (e.g. building consensus; appreciation, acknowledgment)

___ Coaching skills; effective empowerment of people

3. Vision

___ Creating and articulating a future for people

Day 5: Self-Awareness → Basics

Date:_______

It is a good morning exercise
for a research scientist
to discard a pet hypothesis
every day before breakfast.
It keeps him young.
Konrad Lorenz

Visitors to the ancient oracle at Delphi were greeted with the words "Know Thyself" chiseled in stone on top of the massive entry gate. Self-knowledge is the foundation of ethical and effective leadership; without that groundwork, talking about such grand leadership topics as charisma or vision or empowerment is frivolous. Devoid of self-awareness, leadership is a castle built on sand. The question is: can you achieve, and cultivate, self-knowledge? Say you're in a difficult meeting with one of your managers, and he really rubs you the wrong way; can you check your own blindspots?

First of all, whenever we make observations, we have to know where we stand. Scientists do so (or should do so) routinely to calculate mechanics: they have to take themselves and their relative vantage point into account. For example, if a physicist wants to determine the speed of the Earth, she needs to be aware that she's making that calculation within a framework called "solar system," which is itself spinning through space. Knowing where you stand is even more important in the arena of leadership where human beings are involved.

Self-awareness is the ability to check—and take responsibility for—your own assumptions, your motives, and your values. At this bottom level of the Pyramid, you achieve self-awareness by stepping back from the action, being still long enough, and asking yourself: Why am I feeling this way? Why am I frustrated? Why is this important to me?

How do you do that? There are many ways: you can ask a colleague for feedback; you can ask yourself: "What am I not seeing?" "What if the opposite were true?" You can meditate, or pray, or read a poem or a philosophical text; you can listen to music or experience a piece of art; or you can simply go for a walk.

Assignment. Ask someone for unvarnished feedback. Encourage them to say what works about you and what does not work about you. (Tip: just listen, don't defend yourself.)

How did you do? Getting feedback is a great way to check your own social awareness: How well does your self-perception match your perception by others? "There's often a big disconnect between how managers think they are doing and how employees think they're doing," said Robert Morgan of Hudson Talent Management. In a 2006 survey, 92 percent of managers told Rasmussen Reports they were doing an "excellent" or "good" job, while only 67 percent of their subordinates thought so. "Most managers don't think they're doing a bad job," said Morgan. "But if you're not getting feedback from your employees on how well you're doing, where else do you get it from?"[4]

Day 6: Self-Awareness → Diagnostics

Date:_______

The greatest need for leadership is in the dark...
It is when the system is changing so rapidly...
that old prescriptions and old wisdoms
can only lead to catastrophe
and leadership is necessary to call people
to the very strangeness of the new world that is being born.
Kenneth Boulding

How do you know that you need to do more work on the Self-Awareness level? Here are some examples:

- You are suffering (e.g. frustrated, irritated, impatient, humiliated).
- You are stubbornly defending a particular solution or way of doing things.
- You get defensive.
- You refuse to take responsibility.

In those moments it makes little difference, or can even do damage, if you plough ahead or butt your head into the wall at one of the higher levels of the Pyramid. When something rubs you the wrong way, it is time for some self-reflection.

Assignment. Recount a recent moment when you felt frustrated and/or defensive.

What was the emotion that immediately preceded your getting frustrated and/or defensive?

What was important to you (what value, what interest, what motive) that you felt was being violated?

How did you do? People who have a handle on the source of their emotions (for example anger, impatience, feeling rejected, sadness) are better leaders. The ability to self-diagnose gives you insight into how you and others tick. Leaders I worked with recounted incidents that caused them frustration; instead of letting their emotions go through with them like a rodeo horse with its rider, they were able to see what came immediately before the emotion and address the root cause.

Day 7: Self-Awareness → Hidden Drivers

Date:_______

You can observe a lot just by watching.
Yogi Berra

The joke goes that a Buddhist monk entered a pizza shop and requested, "Make me one with everything." Once he got his slice, he handed a $20 bill to the proprietor, who pocketed it. The monk was surprised. "Where is my change?" he asked. The response: "Change? Change comes from within."

The shopkeeper was kidding of course, but at a deeper level he was right. Unless you monitor your blind spots, your inner motives that drive your actions, and not least your ego, you are not in charge of change, but move about like a puppet on the strings of others' demands or factors unknown to you. The upshot is that if you can access the drivers of *internal* change, your change process will be much more sustainable.

Unfortunately countless self-proclaimed "leaders" would start right now for some quick fixes. Not so fast, though. This rush to results and riches was precisely one of the key factors that led to the recent financial crisis and economic meltdown.

Before you can make music, you need to tune your instrument. If your piano is not tuned perfectly, you will make but a cacophony. Similarly, you need to tune up, tune yourself before you start leading.

This idea is far from new. Already at the gates of ancient Delphi, a motto greeted visitors who came for the oracle: "Know Thyself." Self-knowledge is the hallmark of leaders; and if you lack a high level of self-awareness, you have no prayer, and no right, of leading or changing the lives of others.

Unfortunately, history, to this day, is full of leaders who did not know their own hidden drivers and did major damage.

- Are your intentions and motives pure, or are you pursuing your own agenda?
- Are you putting your own interests above those of your colleagues?
- Do you have a need to dominate and exert power, or a need to be loved or praised?
- Do you harbor resentments against a colleague and want to lead him/her as a pretext for dominating him/her?
- Are you overly eager, trying to prove something?
- Do you have any assumptions that might get in the way—for example, "he will never change" or "she's broken and needs fixing"?

All of these are manifestations of ego, and you should be alert to your own "stuff" that has nothing to do with leadership or the work at hand.

Many leaders reject introspection as overly soft and time-consuming. But a leader "must account for his ego," says the famous football coach Bill Walsh.

> English is a marvelous language until it comes to the word "ego." We Americans throw that around, using that one word to cover a broad spectrum of meanings: self-confidence, self-assurance, and assertiveness - attributes that most people think of as positive. But there is another side that can wreck a team or an organization. That is being distracted by your own importance. It can come from your insecurity in working with others. It can be the need to draw attention to yourself in the public arena. It can be a feeling that others are a threat to your own territory. These are all negative manifestations of ego, and if you are not alert to them, you get diverted and your work becomes

> diffused. Ego in these cases makes people insensitive to how they work with others and ends up interfering with the real goal of any group efforts.[5]

Assignment. Where in your work/life have you been ego-ridden (arrogant, defensive, vindictive, stubborn)?

What is the underlying fear that your ego is defending against? What are you afraid of giving up?

How did you do? The more leaders can keep their ego in check, the more unstoppable they will be. It's not about what happens to you; it's about how you respond to what happens to you. After all, that's where the term "responsibility" comes from. Can you take full responsibility for your behaviors, for who you are, and for what you do? Can you expand your agenda and take responsibility for the interests of others, instead of merely dominating them and using them as tools for your own wishes? For example, one client wanted to "coach" his daughter to get into the best possible university—until he realized that he was projecting his own desires onto his daughter.

Day 8: Self-Awareness → Fuzzy Thinking

Date:_______

Even if you're on the right track,
you'll get run over if you just sit there.
Yogi Berra

Unless we're trained to do so, most of us do not naturally appreciate how automatic our thinking is; and even if we do, we live with the unrealistic but confident sense that we know already – that we've figured out the way things really are, and done so objectively. Here are the five most common fallacies of fuzzy thinking:[6]

- ***"It's true because I believe it." (Innate egocentrism)*** I assume that what I believe is true, even though I have never questioned the basis of many of my beliefs.
- ***"It's true because we believe it." (Innate sociocentrism)*** I assume that the dominant beliefs within the groups to which I belong are true, even though I have never questioned the basis for many of those beliefs.
- ***"It's true because I want to believe it." (Innate wish fulfillment)*** I believe in, for example, accounts of behavior that put me (or the groups to which I belong) in a positive rather than a negative light, even though I have not seriously considered the evidence for the more negative account. I believe what "feels good," what supports my other beliefs, what does not require me to change my thinking in any significant way, what does not require me to admit that I have been wrong.
- ***"It's true because I have always believed it." (Innate self-validation)*** I have a strong desire to maintain beliefs that I have long held, even though I have not seriously considered the extent to which those beliefs are justified, given the evidence.

- ***"It's true because it's in my selfish interest to believe it." (Innate selfishness)*** I hold fast to beliefs that justify my getting more power, money or personal advantage, even though those beliefs are not grounded in sound reasoning or evidence.

Most of us, most of the time, are not willing or able to go beyond these self-serving beliefs. We're truly the "self-deceived animal." To be a leader, by contrast, means to be self-determined: it requires a high level of competence in questioning your perspective.

Assignment. Think of a particular issue you face and ask yourself: How am I looking at this? What are my assumptions? Am I basing my judgment on information I failed to verify? Might I be biased or blind to beliefs I never questioned before?

How did you do? Intellectual arrogance and complacency can be perilous; it is one key factor that brought down the venerable carmaker General Motors and led to its bankruptcy in 2009. Finance executive Nancy Rottering, who had quit in frustration in 1987, said the attitude at headquarters was, "We're GM. We know everything, we don't need to change." Jumping to conclusions can be perilous not only in business strategy, but also in human interactions. It is generally a good idea to adopt the most favorable interpretation of the action of another person, especially when that action is not easily understandable. (Of course there is no need to be naïve; if a person has intentionally harmed you in the past, the assumption that they might do so again is based on facts and not far-fetched.)

Day 9: Self-Awareness → 5 Types of Power

Date:_______

Power corrupts;
absolute power corrupts absolutely.
Lord Acton

Leaders exert power. If you want to be an ethical and effective co-leader, you should be aware of power—how and where power is exerted. Most importantly, you should be aware in which situations you have power over others, and where others have power over you (or third parties).

We can distinguish five types of power:

- Reward Power
- Expert/Information Power
- Legitimate Power
- Coercive Power
- Referent Power

Let's look at each type in more detail.

Reward Power is the ability leaders have to grant financial, status, and promotional rewards to the organization's human resources. A boss might have reward power; he or she can grant or withhold compensation or perks or favors. A country's government might have reward power over another country's government if it has the power to apply military, economic or diplomatic sanctions. It's important to understand where you exert reward power, because your followers might fawn all over you and say that you are brilliant when in fact it is just your reward power over them that has them say those nice things.

Information power and expert power are both derived from knowledge, expertise, and access to information sources that others do not have. A professor has expert power vis-à-vis his or her students. In turn, your financial analyst has expert or information power over you (and you can only pray that she won't use it against you). Knowledge workers have expert power, since they often know more than their bosses—they take their expert power home with them every night when they leave the office.

Legitimate Power is conferred by the organization itself, not by the person who occupies a particular position. An elected official has legitimate power; but legitimate power need not be democratic. The Pope is elected only by the Cardinals, rather than by all Catholics. Yet, you could say his power is legitimate. A CEO is not elected but appointed, but his or her power is legitimate as long as the appointment happened according to clear and codified rules.

Coercive power is the ability of a leader to force others to do things they would not otherwise do. If someone comes to power not through clear rules but through a coup or by shooting their way into power, they have coercive power. Jerry Rawlings, the former president of Ghana, did that in the 1980s (but later subjected himself to free and fair elections and thus acquired legitimate power). The most colorful example of coercive power is the mafia. But the mafia is not alone: the government enjoys coercive power over its citizens - it can extract taxes from us, and it can send some of us into battle or to prison (in some states it can even have them killed). And managers have the power to force tasks on employees, or fire them if they don't perform certain functions.

Referent power, the final type of power in this typology, derives from the esteem in which a leader is regarded by others. A movie star or a supermodel might enjoy referent power; they get people to do things they would not otherwise do, like put on strange or expensive outfits. But Gandhi also had referent power: he never held office, and the power he had came from his charisma and the power people gave or *referred* to him. In business, the boss's secretary might have very little nominal power, but her or his referent power can be enormous: she or he can control access to the boss.

You have probably figured out by yourself that these types of power are not entirely separate but can overlap. Bill Gates, for example, can have expert power *and* reward power. Arnold Schwarzenegger has referent power, but also, more recently, legitimate power as governator—sorry, governor—of California.

The idea is to make power plays conscious. If you are a manager who intends to empower people - literally, to be a source of their power -it is part of your job description to be cognizant of the clever yet palpable and often destructive games people play to dominate others or avoid domination by others.

Assignment. Where, and with whom, do you exert which kind of power over another person? Who exerts which kind of power over you? What, if anything, do you want to change in terms of power in your relationships?

How did you do? These distinctions of power can overlap. Bill Gates, for example, might exert both expert power and reward power; parents might have legitimate, expert, reward, referent, and even coercive power over their children ("No more watching TV, you're going to bed now, no discussion!"). The more conscious you are of the power you have over others and the power others have over you, the more choice you have as a leader whether and how you wield power.

Day 10: Self-Awareness → Ethical Dilemmas

Date:_______

The illegal we do immediately,
the unconstitutional takes a little longer.
Henry Kissinger

To be fair, today's leaders face a level of complexity unlike any before in human history. They must often juggle competing values. It is one thing to separate right from wrong—we call that temptation. Ever since the Ten Commandments, everybody knows that you shall not steal or kill. Leaders today are often concerned not with mere temptation but with ethical dilemmas, "right-vs.-right" decisions where the superior and the inferior option are nearly indistinguishable.[7]

When you face a right-vs.-right decision, you come face to face with your underlying value system. What do you do if you are a CEO, your shareholders clamor for relentless growth, and your CFO has found a legal way to hide losses that would suppress the stock price if you showed them to the public? What do you do if you are a toy company whose war games are in huge demand by children, but might turn these children into war-mongers or ADD-ridden computer addicts?

We distinguish four ethical dilemmas:

- Individual vs. group
- Truth vs. loyalty
- Long-term vs. short-term
- Justice vs. mercy

Individual vs. Group. Imagine you are an American junior officer fighting in World War II in Europe. You have been captured by the Germans and are alone in your prison cell. The door opens, and another US officer - a senior officer - is thrown into your cell. As soon as the two of you are alone, the

senior officer tells you that he knows some highly classified military secrets, and he is sure he will blurt them out if the Germans torture him tomorrow. To prevent himself from jeopardizing the war effort, he asks you to strangle him.
→ What do you do: kill him to help win the war, or uphold the sanctity of life?

Truth vs. Loyalty. You are in a meeting with your boss, and she tells you that she unfortunately will have to fire a colleague of yours, who happens to be a good friend too. The boss swears you to secrecy because she wants to be the first one to break the news to your friend. As soon as you leave the boss's office, your friend is standing right outside and asks you, "So what did she say? Will I get fired?"
→ What do you do: tell your friend the truth, or be faithful to your promise to your boss?

Long-term vs. Short-term. You are the marketing director of Johnson & Johnson whose baby oil is a highly profitable product bought by millions of people to get a nice tan; but you find out that the baby oil causes skin cancer.
→ What do you do: keep the product on the market (since it's not your problem if people don't use the product for the intended use) and keep making a hefty profit; or take it off the market, foregoing short-term profits in favor of your long-term credibility and brand image?

Justice vs. Mercy. You are a basketball coach, and you have made it clear to the team that players who don't show up for practice will not play in the championship game this weekend. Three players missed practice last night - and they are precisely the three players you most need to win the game.
→ What do you do: Do you make them sit out the game on the bench, for the sake of justice but jeopardizing your victory; or let them play and break your own word?

You can see that these four ethical dilemmas (like the five types of power in Module 1) are not entirely separate. For example, you could frame the basketball coach's dilemma also as a case of individual vs. group. The important thing to take away is that you have to step back from the action and be still long enough to see what your values are and how to prioritize them.

Assignment. Have you ever faced an ethical dilemma? If so, what kind? Tell the story. How did you resolve the ethical dilemma? What value did you have to favor over which other value?

How did you do? As Ponzi schemes and other frauds dominate the headlines, effective leadership is no longer enough, if it ever was. Now, perhaps more than ever, leadership needs to be both effective *and* ethical. If you can see what ethical dilemmas you face, you can set value priorities. In other words, you can decide which value matters more than which other value. This is an intensely personal question that you have to answer based on your personal and cultural background. For example, some cultures put the group (the family, the community, the society) above the individual, while others never question the assumption that your preferences count above all else.

Day 11: Self-Awareness → Stillness

Date:_______

If I am not for myself, who is for me?
And being only for my own self, what am I?
And if not now, when?
Hillel

Stillness is a quality and a behavior virtually overlooked in leaders. The media show them always debating, moving, performing, and acting (in the best sense of the word). Rarely do we see leaders being still. Yet without stillness, leadership is a hollow shell of blind activity; it lacks insight and wisdom - precisely the qualities that seem at a premium when reality is more complex, the stakes are perhaps higher, and the choices harder than ever. Stepping back from day-to-day activities has us go deeper, to the fundamental values that allow us to make the right choices.

And even without momentous choices, the absence of stillness can have deleterious effects on our lives. Many of us complain about being too connected. "People on cell phones are now reachable in their cars on their commute, and time that used to be down time or transition time is time used by employers," says Gerry Sussman, a professor at the School of Urban Studies and Planning at Portland State University. "Electronic communications makes possible a much deeper penetration for the commercial use of anything," he adds, citing as examples unwanted E-mail, phone solicitation made from computer-generated lists and television advertisements. The rush to sell and consume has made quiet time a scarce commodity.

In the past, great leaders, both Western and non-Western, regularly withdrew from the world to be still, reflect, or meditate, so that what was next could reveal itself to them.

Winston Churchill used to sit outside his house most days after lunch, at the edge of the pond he had made with his own hands, thinking, brooding, and watching the ducks. He would not permit himself to be disturbed. He would sit there for hours sometimes, then return to work in a decisive spirit. Mahatma Gandhi sat, fasted, and prayed at his spinning wheel in order to see what was next in his mission to free India. Nelson Mandela spent twenty-seven years of enforced stillness in prison on Robben Island. During that time of isolation, he developed a resolve of steel. Upon his release, Mandela emerged with utmost clarity on what was needed to end apartheid in South Africa.

Each of these leaders both acted and took time to be still on behalf of millions of people who depended on them for wisdom and insight. Each had to find inner clarity, knowing that his decisions would affect countless lives. Just as they did, those of us who would be leaders, whether in politics, industry, or daily life, have to find the silence within ourselves that is conducive to purposeful action.

If you allow periods of stillness in your life, you can calm down and step back, filter out what is merely urgent from what is truly important, reduce stress and burnout, and perhaps find that which is permanent and timeless. Stillness has nothing to do with passivity, but everything with harmony and balance and wisdom.

In a world where ads all over blurt the promise of "24/7" round-the-clock service, where we surf 250 cable channels or the internet through high-speed modems, and where one restaurant in Tokyo actually charges customers by the minute (rather than by the amount consumed), stillness is not a subject found in business journals or leadership books. But leaders not exactly known for their stillness take time out for reflection. Bill Gates, the founder and chief software architect of Microsoft, regularly takes a "think week" away from all his routines, and returns with fresh ideas distilled from reading and exploration, alone and with others. "The idea is to synthesize and focus on priorities - go up to the 15,000-foot level and really think about directions," said a Microsoft spokeswoman.

Even Andy Grove, the leader of Intel, famous for his restlessness and self-confessed paranoia, reflects regularly to foresee trends in his industry. It is in stillness that you will find your way as a leader. No leadership book or course can give enough advice to cover even a fraction of the situations that any leader will encounter. Unless you can be still and access the wisdom and meaning that stillness makes available, you miss out on one of the most valuable leadership tools. So there is my commercial for stillness.

Assignment:

- Walk deliberately for a full 15 minutes, without interruption, giving conscious instructions to each of your muscles for every tiny movement.
- Note your observations. What thoughts did your mind produce? What worked, what didn't work? What did you learn about stillness?
- What practices do you (or will you) use to maximize your own self-reflection? List these practices, and schedule the ones that are most important for your ongoing self-awareness and clarity on a regular basis.

How did you do? Almost anything you do wholeheartedly, with total focus, can give you access to stillness—from eating an apple slowly and deliberately to washing the car, from a conversation with a friend to taking out the garbage, from reading the paper to wandering around, from making a cup of tea to simply sitting. Whether it is doing the dishes and paying complete attention to the warm water swirling around your hands, the sensation and smell of the soap, the clinking of the cutlery against the cups, the brilliance of a dripping glass; or whether it is making love (no comment on the details here, you'll have to experiment and find out yourself), the key is to be there fully, forget about the opportunity costs of what you might be missing out on (since you're here and not there, you're not missing a thing), and to let yourself live right now to the fullest.

Day 12: Self-Awareness → Culture Clash

Date:_______

A hundred times a day, I remind myself
that my inner and outer life depend
on the labors of other men, living and dead.
And that I must exert myself
in order to give in the same measure
as I have received and am still receiving.
Albert Einstein

One final but all-important facet of self-awareness is the ability to see your own cultural blind-spots, and to decode other cultures and value-systems.[8]

What happens if you disregard the Global Leader Pyramid®? "Without the least bit of *Schadenfreude* (an untranslatable German word for glee at the damage of others), I recall my prediction in a speech in mid-1999 that the merger of Mercedes and Chrysler would fall on its face. The writing was on the wall: just ten months after the merger that created DaimlerChrysler, the American top executive in charge of integrating the operations in Stuttgart with those in Auburn Hills resigned. Though touting DaimlerChrysler as a "merger of equals," Europeans dominated the new entity from the start. Co-chairman Jürgen Schrempp put himself firmly in charge, pushed all but two Americans from the management board of the combined company and installed his trusted German aide Dieter Zetsche at Chrysler's helm." (Thomas D. Zweifel, *Culture Clash 2.0*)

In order to produce an accomplishment of size, a project must move through four stages: relationship, vision, strategy, and action. National and regional culture differ in their emphasis on these levels. If managers fail to respect the cultural emphasis on a particular level, cultures will inevitably clash. [Note: countries are chosen as illustrations only, and represent approximations of real situations.]

Fig. 2: Building Global Results

What went wrong? Jürgen Schrempp, DaimlerChrysler's CEO at the time, ignored every level of the Pyramid: In Self-Awareness, he failed to see the cultural differences between the German and American companies. At the Relationship level, he rebuffed an invitation by the Chrysler board to meet with them, and instead chose to go on an ill-timed vacation on his South African ranch; and the joint management board consisted of 16 Germans and 2 Americans. In Vision, he failed to integrate the disparate visions of Daimler ("Only the Best," i.e. top quality, with the customer's wishes as an afterthought) and Chrysler (whatever designs work for the customer). In Strategy, he failed to build a shared understanding or a joint strategic plan; Daimler refused to give diecasting designs to Chrysler's managers for fear that the Americans wouldn't understand them.

On the Action level, the bill came due eventually: "DaimlerChrysler paid dearly for this new brand of German imperialism. At the time of this writing, the company's revenue was to fall by 13 percent and operating profits as much as 75 percent in 2001, forcing it to eliminate 26,000 jobs and suffer major brain drain from the loss of some of Chrysler's most creative talent." (Thomas D. Zweifel, *Culture Clash*) Today, Chrysler has been bought by Fiat and DaimlerChrysler is history.

Assignment. Research the DaimlerChrysler case, e.g. on Google: Where were the Chrysler culture and the Daimler culture compatible, and where not?

How did you do? Carlos Ghosn, who was born in Brazil, raised in Lebanon, and is a citizen of France, might serve as a counter-example to Schrempp. In 1999, he was sent to Japan by France's Renault S.A. when the company had bought 36.8% of Nissan. His mission: to restructure and revive the ailing Japanese car manufacturer. His promise: to post a profit for the fiscal year ending in March 2001. His process entailed closing factories, axing thousands of jobs and cutting off small, money-losing affiliates would have hardly endeared Ghosn to the Japanese, who are not exactly open to foreign managers. But the improbable happened: Ghosn succeeded, his autobiography sold 150,000 in the first month, and he has even become a comic book star—probably the highest honor in comic-crazed Japan. He eventually became the chief of Renault. (In 2018 Japanese authorities arrested him amid allegations of false accounting; as of this writing these alleged crimes remained unproven in court. Even if Ghosn were convicted, that would not invalidate his accomplishments at Nissan.) What was Ghosn's main recipe for success? He recognized the power of building trust and involving your global partners in your vision and strategy.

Day 13: Self-Awareness → Decoding Cultures

Date:_______

The real voyage of discovery consists
not in seeking new landscapes
but in having new eyes.
Marcel Proust

How can you avoid such cross-cultural mistakes and their strategic consequences? The simplest tool for decoding a culture (of a corporation or a country) is the so-called "onion model" developed by the father of cultural anthropology, Geert Hofstede and refined by Fons Trompenaars (Trompenaars and Hampden-Turner 1997). You can distinguish three layers of culture.

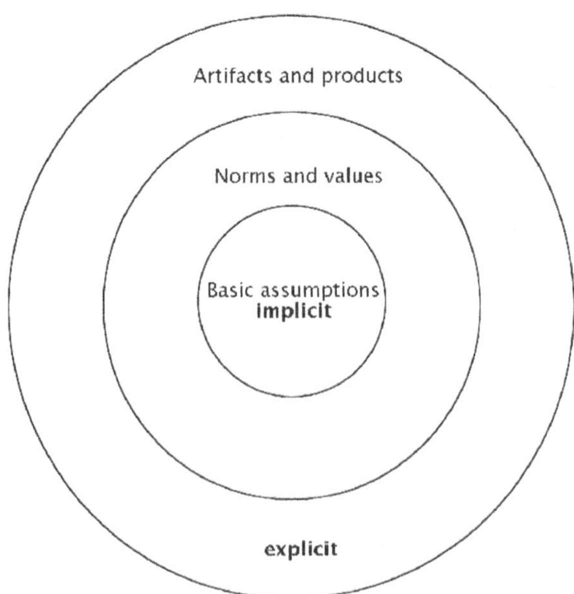

Fig. 3: The Onion Model of Culture

The most apparent—the outside layer—are the explicit, visible and audible artifacts, products, signals and behaviors you can readily observe, for example logos, dress codes, architecture, movies, or how people eat. An example would be that people in Japan who are sick put on a surgical mask in public.

The second layer are the norms and values in a culture, including how people justify and rationalize the first layer: "The way we do things around here is... because..." In our example of Japan, people might say, "We don't want to infect anyone on our small island where so many people live so close together."

The third and innermost layer—the core—is what I would call the actual culture: the past decisions that have become so automatic as to become invisible, even unconscious. What is it that people don't even know they don't know? These are the basic assumptions or blind-spots: in other words, the culture. For example, in Japan, harmony, respect and relationship are basic assumptions in the culture.

Now, how do you decode this innermost, invisible culture? An elegant way involves three facets.

#1: Understand the ideology and values of the Founders and Heroes. The myth of William Tell, who ambushed the Hapsburg vassal Gessler and catalyzed a movement to throw out the Hapsburgs and found Switzerland, is telling, if we want to understand, why Switzerland jealously guards its neutrality and has steadfastly refused to join the United Nations or the European Union. The founders of the United States enshrined their values of life, liberty and the pursuit of happiness, which are underpinnings of U.S. culture. (By contrast, no European constitution contains such a fundamental right to pursue happiness.) To understand Israel, you would want to learn about David Ben Gurion and Golda

Meir. Learning about them would tell you a lot about the Israeli culture.

#2: Identify Villains and Outcasts. Another facet in decoding a culture is to **see who are the "villains" or outcasts** - in other words, what behaviors are not permissible, even taboo, in the dominant culture. For example, when I was in Cuba, I saw how the Latin machismo culture, including the state, oppresses and ridicules homosexuals. In the U.S. culture, atheism is permissible, but atheists find themselves clearly outside the mainstream and are suspect to the mainstream. It is rare for politicians to win political office unless they vociferously and repeatedly reaffirm their belief in God - which is usually not a requirement for politicians in most other countries.

#3: Identify Defining Moments in shaping the culture. The third step is to look through the history of a culture and identify wars and other (for instance economic) crises that are often defining moments in shaping a culture. For example, the first and second world wars helped shape a self-understanding of the U.S. culture that America is always the good guy fighting against the bad guys in the effort of saving the world. Wilson declared that the U.S. was fighting World War I to "make the world safe for democracy." By its entry into World War II, the United States prevented Nazi Germany's world dominance.

Both wars ended the Monroe Doctrine, which in 1823 had stated the United States' intention to stay neutral in European wars and in wars between European powers and their colonies. But by 1944, the United States actively espoused a new role - that of saving the world (from Nazism, then from Communism, and most recently from terrorism). From then on, it saw itself as a benevolent hegemon, imposing democracy in Germany and Japan, going to war in Korea and Vietnam and the Persian Gulf, underwriting much of the UN system, monitoring elections in Zambia, etc. This noble stance has had countless beneficial effects; take just the Marshall Plan, in which the United States sponsored the reconstruction of Europe after the war, or the fact that it pays for about one-quarter of the entire budget of the United Nations and its multilateral agencies. But at the same time, its commitment to help the world has at times turned the United States into a global policeman and has pitted it against those who felt that it was exerting undue influence in the internal affairs of other countries. For better or for worse, "We know what is good for the world" has become an unquestioned cultural assumption not only in U.S. foreign policy, but also in U.S. multinationals.

Assignment. Cause a specific, targeted, tangible change through a cross-cultural interaction. Preferably you would do this with a colleague in another country; but if you don't work with people in other countries, you could still have a cross-cultural interaction with someone from another racial background, another social class, or even another department within your organization (e.g. someone in operations if you are in sales). Use the Onion model above to decode the other person's culture as well as your own; then have the interaction. (For example, you may want a colleague from another culture and/or country to keep his/her time commitments, or to deepen your working relationship, or to give you honest feedback on how they perceive you and your work, or to lead the next conference call.)

Debrief the experience: what did you accomplish? What did you not accomplish? What worked, what did not work in the interaction?

Another, fun way of decoding a culture is by its proverbs. Here some random examples:

- Bulgarian: Friendship is friendship but cheese costs money.
- Colombian: Eat and drink, because life is brief.
- Indian: If you can kill someone with sugar, why use poison?

- Kazakh: Measure seven times, cut once.
- Pakistani: Do not stand up to get the attention of someone who did not notice you when you were sitting.
- Swiss: He who does not honor the Rappen (penny) is not worth the Franken (dollar).

Assignment. What are three proverbs you know, and what does each of them say about the culture from which the proverb stems?

How did you do? On the change management front, the cross-cultural change might be small; for example, the fact that a colleague from another culture does not clean up in the office kitchen might bother you. On the proverb front, for example the Swiss proverb, "He who does not honor the Rappen (penny) is not worth the Franken (dollar)" says a lot about Swiss frugality, which probably originated with the Reformation (the Protestant aversion to the opulence of the Catholic church) and Swiss attention to detail (to put it mildly).

Day 14: Relationship → The Basics

Date:_______

Out beyond ideas of wrongdoing and rightdoing,
there is a field. I will meet you there.
When the soul lies down in that grass,
the world is too full to talk about.
Ideas, language, even the phrase "each other"
doesn't make any sense.
Rumi

Now that we have completed the level of Self-knowledge in the Pyramid, we can move up to the second level: Relationship.

Assignment. Before you begin this module, see how you can apply the information from Days 1-13 to your 100-Day Catalytic Project. You have now put 13 days behind you, so please take stock of where you are:

What results have I seen?

What have I learned?

What worked?

What didn't work?

What's next to reach my 100-Day Catalytic Project goal?

We are now ready to proceed. The Relationship level may sound trivial, but all too many leaders (especially in Western cultures) bypass it altogether and try to get right down to business. Those who do appreciate its importance often think that having a beer (or a few beers) with colleagues after hours is enough. We have seen that true Relationship goes much deeper: it's about building partnership and trust with the allies you need to get the job done.

Often, managers respond at one of the higher levels of the Pyramid (Vision, Strategy, Action) when they should really take care of the Relationship level. If one of your direct reports is late for the Monday morning staff meeting, you could say that she failed to keep her agreement, which is an Action item; in that case, your response might be, "Please don't be late next time." But it could well be that the direct report was late because he/she is not sufficiently owning the vision or strategy, or not fully related to the project at hand. If you go back to the Relationship level and build from there, you will get at the root cause of the person's lateness, rather than merely fighting the symptoms.

The broader and deeper your relationships, the higher and more sustainable you can build the Pyramid (i.e., your desired accomplishment). By contrast, if you have a tiny base of Relationship, your Pyramid and accomplishments will be tiny too.

So how do you build relationships of trust, shared values, and shared commitments? The simple answer is: through communication. And what questions do you ask to build an extraordinary working relationship that can yield extraordinary results? Here are some questions that work (feel free to experiment with others):

- Who are you? Where are you from? What is your background?
- What are your core values?
- What can I count on you for? What can you count on me for?
- What interests or commitments do we have in common?
- How might our work together further your/my commitments?

How did you do? It's important that you take stock of your results and learnings before moving up to the higher levels of the Pyramid. They give you useful data that you can use for the higher levels. And if you didn't get very far yet, don't worry: It lies in the nature of the beast. So far you have focused on the foundation of the Pyramid, Self-Awareness. Once this groundwork is solidly in place, you will be able to build accomplishments with ease and pace.

Day 15: Relationship → Diagnostics

Date:_______

The greatest problem about communication is the illusion that it has been accomplished.
George Bernard Shaw

How do you know that Relationship is too weak or missing altogether? The symptoms include:

- People are upset. This is a surefire way to recognize that Relationship is missing.
- People are not expressing themselves, they are holding back.
- People are not talking straight with each other; they are exceedingly polite with each other.
- The opposite: people are exceedingly impolite and rude with each other.
- People repeatedly decline requests.

Assignment. Work on strengthening the Relationship level with someone in your work life, preferably someone who is also impacted or involved with your 100-Day Catalytic Project. Rate the quality of the relationship with that person (not the person!) from 1 to 10, 1 being the weakest, 10 the strongest relationship. Write your criteria for your rating of that relationship. Identify what is missing that would allow you to rate the relationship higher (ideally at a 10). Contact the person in question and begin building an effective working relationship characterized by trust, shared values, shared commitments, and shared interests.

How did you do? At times doing this exercise may feel a bit awkward or mechanical; it's as if you were learning a new sport and using a muscle in your body that you never used before, and it feels strange. It may even seem that it works less well than what you're used to. I have one word for you: Practice. Learning the art and science of building and cultivating relationships is like learning to play the violin: Before you can make beautiful music, you have to practice the same chords over and over, and at first you make a lot of dissonant noises. It's part of the game.

Day 16: Relationship → Building Trust

Date:_______

The best way to find out
if you can trust somebody
is to trust them.
Ernest Hemingway

The ground rule is that the broader and deeper the foundation of your relationships, the higher you can build the Pyramid of accomplishment. Without at least some basic trust, you cannot build a meaningful accomplishment—a point easily lost on most of the Western world in which the court system has largely replaced a system of trust based on Relationship.

The management consultant and "philosopher of language" (as *Fast Company* magazine called him) Fernando Flores knows a lot about trust—and its absence. At twenty-nine, he became minister of finance—one of the youngest in any country—in Salvador Allende's government in Chile. After the government was overthrown in a bloody military coup, Flores was jailed. He found himself utterly betrayed by the country he loved and had served. He was sent to prison without a trial, and faced execution several times while his wife and five children waited anxiously. It is difficult to imagine a more trust-shattering experience. But in the face of prison and possibly imminent execution, Flores came to realize that the first and most important ingredient in trust is *self*-trust, and the unwavering trust of and in those people closest to you. Flores's three years in prison gave him crystal clarity on trust and the power it provides.

More and more managers work on or through virtual teams, do business via the Internet, or outsource activities to back-office operations elsewhere in the country or across the planet.

If you take away the new technology, virtual teams are nothing new, by the way.

Wherever information is the raw material of work, it has never been necessary to have all the people in the same place at the same time: take a network of salespeople, or a team of newspaper reporters. These teams are so common that we would never think of giving them such a grandiose title as "virtual organization." Yet they are.

More and more knowledge workers (as the management theorist Peter Drucker calls them) work with the information and know-how they have. Over time, organizations will likely be forced to cut the costs of maintaining real offices wherever they can (it's not cost-effective to have an office available 168 hours a week but occupied for, say, 30 hours.)

The confluence of economics and technology means that more and more managers will spend time in virtual space—out of sight, if not out of touch.

So how do you manage people whom you do not see? The simple answer is, by trusting them. You can't tell free agents what to do, so command-and-control techniques of management don't cut it anymore. Virtual teams require trust—more trust even than the usual teams who see each other every day.

And how do you build trust? As the British management theorist Charles Handy puts it, "high tech has to be balanced by high touch to build high-trust organizations."

Ultimately, you build trust by making and keeping commitments. If you promise me something and deliver on your promise, large or small, that builds trust.

Assignment. Have a conversation with a co-worker or loved one that builds trust between you. (Tip: A simple way to build trust is to make a commitment and keep that commitment.) What are your observations? Specifically, what worked and what did not work in building trust?

How did you do? Once you have done the assignment, you can increase the difficulty, either by building trust with someone you don't see because they are not in the same office, or with someone from a different culture and mindset than your own, or with someone you don't quite get along with. You may even want to ask each of these people how they would rate the trust between you, and then negotiate a "contract" with mutual promises the keeping of which will upgrade the level of trust.

Day 17: Relationship → The Power of Listening

Date:_______

The tongue weighs practically nothing.
But so few people can hold it.
Anonymous

Before you open your mouth (or worse, before you say something you may regret later), open your ears and listen actively. This module is about how you can listen effectively and in a way that causes new levels of results.

One chief executive, reminded of the importance of two-way communication, snapped: "*Of course* I use two-way communication! I communicate to my people both verbally and in writing!" (He of course meant "orally," not verbally.) Unfortunately, this executive is not alone in ignoring the dimension of listening. Nobody seems to listen anymore; instead, talk abounds in our society. Day and night we are inundated with infomercials and e-mail broadcasts urging us to buy this or try that.

It seems that everyone has something to say. When people tell others to "listen," they really mean "shut up" so they can say their brilliant thing. Especially in the Western culture, the important people talk, while those who have nothing to say listen. Listening is so invisible that it goes virtually unrecognized. Listening makes no noise, is intangible, and leaves little evidence, while talk is loud, gets attention, and can be recorded.

Although listening is a fundamental skill, we are not taught how to do it. There are very few how-to books and virtually no schools on listening skills. There are debating clubs and championships for orators, but no showcases or awards for excellent listeners.

But listening is not just a nice thing to do or a soft skill. Imagine a company with seven reporting levels. If the people at every level report 50% of what they know up to the next higher level - and 50% is a rather optimistic number – the leader at the top will know 1.6% of what is actually going on.

If control resides solely at the top, the consequences of being that out of touch can be disastrous for decision-making. Imagine what happens if the leader happens to base his or her decisions on the 98.4% of irrelevant information. In today's complex and fast-changing organizations, chief executives depend on vital strategic information from others, both within the organization and from outside it. Listening is a crucial vehicle for getting that strategic intelligence.

Listening also allows you to find great talent. If you talk ceaselessly, you will never find out what other people think, who they are, or the added value they bring to the team. If, on the other hand, you ask some targeted questions (like "Who are you?" or "What is your vision, what do you want in life?" or "What is missing in our strategy that you can provide?"), you will be able to recruit the best people.

Assignment. Experiment with listening in your life and work, e.g. in meetings, on conference calls, or at the dinner table. What happens if you ask a question and then shut up?

How did you do? In my former life as an executive, I realized that I was too dominant on our global conference calls. My colleagues were either too diplomatic to say so, or they were glad that I was taking the lead so they didn't have to. So I decided to do an experiment: I would come to the conference calls not with my agenda or speaking points, but with one or two key questions, and then I would listen. At first my colleagues were a bit dumbfounded: When would I take over again? But as they got used to having the privilege and responsibility of co-leadership, they got going. And the calls became a true co-creation. It made my job easier; and it was a factor in the global team's generation of a breakthrough result: increasing revenue at a 45% compound rate over 5 years while keeping expenses stable.

Day 18: Relationship → Anger Management

Date:_______

I have learned through bitter experience
the one supreme lesson to conserve my anger,
and as heat conserved is transmuted into energy,
even so our anger controlled can be transmuted
into a power which can move the world.
Mahatma Gandhi

Listening also plays an important role in anger management. When a colleague seems to sabotage you or things don't go your way, do you blow up and throw a temper tantrum, or can you step back and listen one minute longer?

Mahatma Gandhi was able to listen even to his enemies instead of getting angry. The late Ramkrishna Bajaj, the Indian industrialist who as a young man had worked as "Gandhi's coolie," as he wrily put it in the title of his autobiography) told me a story about Gandhi. One of his followers, Dr. Manibhai Desai, had been a militant anarchist in India's underground movement as a young man and knew India's jails from the inside. Later, however, he came to embrace Gandhi's nonviolent ways.

From 1942 onward, Desai served as Gandhi's assistant and for a while was in charge of answering all the letters that came to the independence leader. And since there were virtually no telephones in India and no email for decades to come, Gandhi received an enormous amount of mail - including heaps of hate mail. Desai feared that the vengeful letters would only distract Gandhi from his mission of nonviolence, and decided to shield his leader from all the negativity. He hid the bad letters and quietly answered them himself.

But Gandhi must have smelled that something was amiss. One day he gently prodded Desai, "I seem to be getting only nice letters lately. Where are the critical ones?" Blushing slightly, Desai admitted that he had kept the hate mail from Gandhi. He was never to forget Gandhi's answer until he died in 1993. "I need the negative letters," said the great leader. "My critics are my best friends. They show me what I have still to learn."

Here are some basic listening tips:

- Focus on them, not on yourself.
- Put your tendency to evaluate on hold.
  Mentally recreate what they're saying. Take notes if necessary.
- See things from their point of view.
- Listen for the "gold"—not the garbage.
- Listen one minute longer than may be comfortable.
- Experiment with listening. What results could you cause purely by the way you listen to other people? What if you produced three times your current results simply by listening?
- Remember that your advice is noise in their ears.

Assignment. Describe a recent incident where you had an intense negative emotion (anger, envy, fear).

How did you use listening to regulate your emotion?

What worked, what didn't work?

What practices do (will) you use to regulate your emotions?

How did you do? When you feel an intense emotion like anger and somehow find the discipline not to react like a barking dog, and instead listen a bit longer than might be comfortable, some new opening or empathy or insight might emerge and the emotion might subside or change into something else. Try it.

Day 19: Relationship → Listening for Subtexts

Date:_______

Listen! Or your tongue will make you deaf.
Cherokee saying

You may have noticed yesterday that the distinction we drew is between listening *to* and listening *for*. When you listen to the content of another person's speaking, you are listening to the "text." But if you want to listen actively, you have to train yourself to listen *for* the "subtexts."

Listening *to* the **text**	Listening *for* the **subtexts**

According to the German communication psychologist Friedemann Schulz von Thun, there are three sub-texts in virtually any communication. These are listed in the table.

3 Subtexts in any Communication
• **Appeal** (the speaker wants, implicitly or explicitly, wittingly or unwittingly, to influence a situation; he or she wants something). • **Self-disclosure** (the speaker implies something about him- or herself, his or her mood or feeling or thought); • **Relating** (the speaker implies how he or she stands vis-à-vis the listener, what they think about the listener); and

When my late mother asked my late father, "Aren't you cold?", there were several sub-texts that my mother may or may not have been conscious of:

- The appeal was, "Shut the window please" or "Give me your sweater."

- The self-disclosure was, "I am cold myself" or "I feel helpless."
- The relating was, "I care about you" or "You're my husband, you could pay more attention to me."

By listening actively and training your muscle to hear not only the factual content but the sub-texts of any communication, you will be much more equipped to deal effectively with any communication. You will be in charge of the conversation. You will be an effective communicator.

Assignment. Recall a moment when a colleague, family member or friend of yours told you a "brick-wall statement," for example, "Why am I always the one who has to stay long hours and do the stuff that everybody else dumps on me? Couldn't someone else do something for a change?"
Listen for the facts in the statement; then listen for the three sub-texts (self-disclosure, relating, and appeal).
List your observations of each of the sub-texts. (Hint: trust your intuition.)

Listen to at least one person (a colleague or friend or family member) tell a story.
First, listen to the content (the text) of the story. At the same time, see if you can identify the sub-texts in the story (self-disclosure, relating, and appeal).

How did you do? Great customer service reps and consummate sales people, but also transcendent sports coaches like Phil Jackson, know instinctively that simply talking about how great your company or product or team is doesn't cut the mustard. If on the other hand they listen for the subtext, they can address concerns of customers or players that might be hidden to other people. And by doing that, they can unlock hidden potentials of the people they serve or coach.

Day 20: Relationship → Masterful Listening

Date:_______

Knowledge speaks, but wisdom listens.
Jimi Hendrix

Most people have a mechanistic, black-and-white understanding of listening. At best they treat listening like a light switch to turn on and off, and fail to see the rich body of distinctions listening can be. But much like painting or strategy, listening is a complex art—one that takes sustained effort to develop, but yields surprising results to those who dare to make it a life-long quest.

Listening produces real effects. You can make or break people by the way you listen to them. When Oprah Winfrey listens to guests on her show, she - or more precisely, her empathy—turns ordinary people into fascinating human beings. Winfrey says that her emotional connection to her guests is a way of relating to people that grew when she was a television news reporter. She explains, "You're at a plane crash and you're smelling the charred bodies, and people are coming to find out if their relatives are in the crash and they're weeping, and you weep too because it's a tragic thing."[9] The same empathetic listening that made Winfrey cry while reporting the news made her an instant success as a talk-show host and one of the wealthiest and most powerful media leaders.

Just as listening to others can embolden and enable them, not listening can damage a person's spirit and effectiveness. We have seen people's initiative crushed, performance break down, or mergers go awry—all because of poor communication and listening skills. In a survey of 22,000 shift workers in various U.S. industries, 70 percent stated that they have little communication with plant and company management, and 59 percent said that their companies do not care about them—which is another way of saying that nobody listens to them. You can make or break someone with the power of your listening.

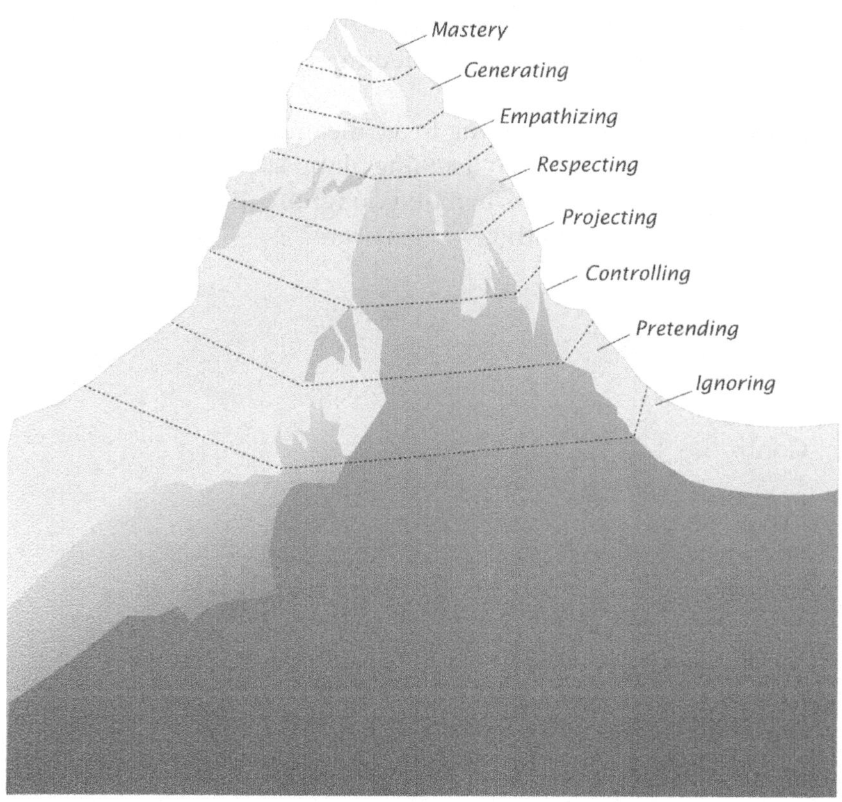

Fig.4: Matterhorn of Masterful Listening

Here are the definitions for each level of the Matterhorn of Masterful Listening™:

1. Ignoring = Absence of listening
2. Pretending = Appearing to listen when you really don't (Ignoring with hypocrisy).

3. Controlling = Influence (through body language, facial expressions, sounds, or authority) what the speaker can say.
4. Projecting = Listening through the filter of your own prior beliefs or judgments. Hearing what you want to hear.
5. Respecting = Hearing the content of what is actually said.
6. Empathizing = Listening for the speaker's intention.
7. Generating = Listening for the speaker's brilliance/leadership. Listening for the gold.
8. Mastery = Listening to the listening.

Assignment. While listening to a colleague, friend or family member, check your own listening along the Matterhorn of Masterful Listening™: when do you ignore, pretend, control, project, respect, empathize, or generate?

Ignore:

Pretend:

Control:

Project:

Respect:

Empathize:

Generate:

Take an organizational challenge (either within your 100-Day Catalytic Project or distinct from it) and apply the Matterhorn of Masterful Listening™ to it. See if you can produce three times your current results through the quality of your listening.

How did you do? Many readers of *Communicate or Die* and participants in "Communicate or Die" workshops discover that they tend to gravitate toward a certain level of listening in their key relationships. For example, they might routinely be Pretending to listen with that talkative colleague; or if that doesn't do the job, they might use Controlling by looking at their watch or saying, "This better be quick, I have a meeting to run to."

By the way, the higher levels of the Matterhorn of Masterful Listening™ are not necessarily better than the lower ones. The bottom level, Ignoring, can be appropriate for certain situations, for example unwanted sales calls or spam emails. The trick is to choose consciously and deliberately at which level you intend to listen, instead of leaving it to chance or to fickle moods.

Day 21: Relationship → Speaking

Date:_______

The ability to speak is what marks man as man.
This mark contains the design of his being.
Man would not be man
if it were denied him to speak unceasingly,
from everywhere and every which way,
in many variations…
Language, in granting all this to man,
is the foundation of human being.
Martin Heidegger

Now that we have examined and toned our listening muscle, we can move on to the more visible aspect of communication: speaking. At the start of this WorkBook, we saw that leaders are people who have certain conversations: effective conversations of value that empower people to produce desired results. But all too often, leaders and managers sabotage their own efforts by unproductive, wasteful, or toxic speaking that escalates issues and can lead to discord, divorce, failed mergers, lawsuits and even war. Speaking irresponsibly is among the most counterproductive things people can do. I call such speaking "ontological pollution," which can be at least as damaging as environmental pollution. Dumping blame or judgment on someone is just as bad as dumping a Coke bottle out of the car window.

The capital sins of unproductive speaking are rumor; judgment; excuse; and threat. These types of speaking have two things in common: they do damage, and they stifle action. The damage is often done unwittingly. When the financial controller at one of our dot-com clients says in frustration, "I can't pay the bills as long as those account executives don't produce sales," her intentions are good. She is even right. But people around her do not experience any opening for action from her threat. All they experience is guilt and blame.

Capital Sin #1: Rumor. Our first sin of speaking is usually about the personal affairs of others. A French phrase aptly sums up this way of speaking: *"Les absents ont toujours tort"* ("Those who are gone are always wrong"). The French got it exactly right: rumor and gossip are never communicated directly to the people whom they badmouth. They are at the opposite end of the spectrum from responsibility.

Rumor and gossip rise with bad times, so expect more of them in this next phase of economic uncertainty. The more people sense that their job is on the line, the less straight they will be to your face. Fear will block them from communicating honestly. At one client I worked with, people had never been trained to say what they thought to each other's faces. In public, they said only the words they thought their superiors wanted to hear. Two people, the chairman and the CEO, took it to the extreme. Each of them called their consultant overseas—each separately—to talk about the other, when their offices were about a three-minute walk apart.

Rumor and gossip include complaining about an issue to people who have no power to do something about it. Most of us have that nasty habit. We complain to anyone and everyone except the person who can do something to resolve our complaint. If you are an account executive, complaining to other account executives about the VP of sales will only aggravate your issue, because all you do is gather evidence for your viewpoint instead of speaking to the VP directly. The person who complains only to co-workers who cannot act fuels the perception that "nothing matters," "we have no power to change things," "they never listen," or "life here sucks."

Deadly Sin #2: Judgment. In 1997, David Risher, a fast-rising young Microsoft executive, decided to join an intriguing Internet startup called Amazon.com. Risher's direct superior at

Microsoft asked him incredulously: "You're going to leave Microsoft for a *retailer*?" When Risher was undeterred, he was summoned to Bill Gates' office. He remembers how the Microsoft founder told him quitting was "the stupidest decision you'll ever make." Gates had committed the sin of judgment, and he was dead wrong. Today, Risher is head of all US retail operations and one of Amazon's top ten executives. He is worth around $100 million—*after* the Amazon stock slump.

Webster gives us several meanings for judgment, including "the ability to judge, make a decision, or form an opinion objectively, authoritatively, and wisely." In this book judgment has quite the opposite meaning. It is the act of giving our opinions or conclusions in a way that is subjective, invalid, or short-sighted. We judge: "She's too emotional." "He's pushy." "The Web developers just don't get it." "This CEO will never change." "The stupidest decision you'll ever make."

Are you limiting what somebody can do by the very way you characterize them? As an effective leader you must avoid jumping to quick, stereotypical judgments about others. It's not okay to judge people as persons. Judging people's actions is better, but still risky. If possible, avoid judgment altogether and instead talk about your experience. "I had the experience of being bypassed by you when you scheduled that meeting without informing me. I know it probably was not your intention, but that was my experience."

Deadly Sin #3: Excuse. An excuse is an explanation or defense that one offers as a reason not to be held accountable. Your business development manager says, "I didn't deliver last month's sales goal because I got the specs from the Web developers too late." "We did our best under the circumstances. What else do you want us to do?" Rationalizing, a close cousin of excuses, implies self-deception and even denial. We rationalize to avoid confronting the truth. "Sure, we knew that software wasn't up to company standards. But what could we do? Management wanted it out by Christmas."

Excuses and rationalizations are unproductive for two reasons. First, they are attempts to deflect responsibility by making the speaker look like a victim of overwhelming circumstances. The French language offers an apt description of this aspect of excuses: *Qui s'excuse, s'accuse* ("Those who excuse themselves accuse themselves" - though it sounds way more elegant in French). Second, they over-emphasize the past, generally in an attempt to free us from blame. The problem is, they perpetuate the past: they give us little chance of creating a future that differs from that past.

Deadly Sin #4: Threat. When your back is against the wall and you see no other method of getting your way, you might resort to the fourth sin of speaking: you threaten an ultimatum. "If this doesn't change, you can always sack me... I'm thinking of leaving anyway." I know a CEO who used to issue this type of ultimatum about every two weeks. Threats are really a sign of weakness, though. They put your listeners on notice that you are on the defensive—not a very smart tactic for a leader. And they create a lot of unnecessary adversity. You separate yourself from everybody else on the team, and you make people see you as an *enfant terrible* that shouldn't be taken seriously.

How do you reveal, and avoid, unnecessary clutter in your speaking, and turn wasteful communication into committed, future-oriented speech that produces the changes you want? One way is this: As you go through your day, think of every statement you say or hear as a commitment. If you catch yourself saying things like "Nobody wants to buy this product" or "I don't trust that guy," ask yourself: am I committed to that interpretation?

Assignment. Catch yourself at one of the four capital sins of speaking (a rumor, complaint, blame, or excuse) and turn it into a commitment.

Assignment. Observe brick-wall statements in your life / work (e.g. "You never listen to me!" or "They made the decision—now they can deal with the consequences" or "Why do I always have to do the bulk of the work?") and turn them into future-based conversations.

How did you do? The capital sins of speaking (a rumor, complaint, blame, or excuse) are often expressions of victimhood. People complain, for example, when they feel that the circumstances are stronger than they, and that they can't do anything, so they talk to someone who will commiserate, or whine, or reproach, or justify why they can't get the job done. A simple way to move from such sins of speaking to responsibility and commitment is to ask the person, "What is your promise or request?"

Day 22: Relationship → Appreciation Is Power

Date:_______

The most intolerable state for human beings
is not to be acknowledged.
William James

Appreciation—a key to building and deepening Relationship—is not a favor you do someone, but a fundamental human need and a powerful tool of leadership.

Nobody ever left a company because they were too appreciated. On the other hand, if you don't value your people, the costs can be enormous. A decade ago, Procter & Gamble, plagued by an attrition rate twice as high for women than for men, asked the women it saw as "regretted losses" - high performers it wanted to keep - why they had left. The simple answer was that they did not feel valued. "Many said they didn't realize they were regretted losses until they were contacted for the survey," said Jeannie Tharrington, a P&G spokeswoman.

Deloitte & Touche had an even greater revelation when it surveyed women on the partner track who had quit the firm in the 1990s. "It turned out that more than ninety percent of them were still employed, just not by us," recalled Cathleen A. Benko, who runs Deloitte's high-tech sector and its Initiative for the Retention and Advancement of Women. "So much for the idea that women stay home to run families."

If you calculate the training and HR costs for one executive at around $1 million, you can imagine the costs of such under-appreciation. If you fail to appreciate somebody, it is as if you were stealing from them - but also from yourself.

One of these women leaders was forty-eight-year-old Zara F. Larsen, who learned long ago to use e-mail messaging and telecommuting to juggle family responsibilities and work. She rotated through four major assignments in ten years at United Technologies. In 2004, she felt her career had reached a plateau, and quit to pursue a doctorate in management. "I was no longer getting the intellectual stimulation I needed," she said.

But an "irresistible" offer from Raytheon Missile Systems wooed Larsen back to the corporate world: take time to pursue your degree, the company said, but also be our director of enterprise effectiveness, responsible for shrinking costs, speeding up processes and otherwise changing the culture.

Unfortunately this power of appreciation is—surprise!—not appreciated. Familiarity breeds contempt: we tend to take for granted the people that we see every day, whether our families or our employees or our leaders. In 2002, I was in Berlin when the German national soccer team achieved the superb feat of reaching the finals of the World Cup; but I heard not a single word of appreciation from the Germans watching the championship performance. The highest compliment was "Well, they could have done better." Not a climate in which people want to give their best.

But we don't have to look in Germany; let's start right in our own backyard. Most of us see mostly what's wrong, we complain, or we think the grass is always greener on the other side. We are like Not-Enough Machines: when was the last time you woke up and said, "Last night I had enough sleep"? We don't have enough time or money, our bodies are not beautiful or young enough, we don't have enough friends or security or love - and the list goes on.

Remember that appreciation means both acknowledgment *and* increase in value. If you have a colleague or a situation that bugs you, perhaps you can find it in yourself to appreciate them, or at least to appreciate why they were put into your path. What can you learn from the situation? What side of you does the obnoxious colleague activate?

Some people savor a glass of wine more than their life accomplishment... One coaching client, a senior executive, was so unconscious and automatic with his disparaging thoughts and comments—about himself, his job, or the CEO who was his boss—that he, unwittingly but incessantly, sabotaged himself and his work. To exercise and build his muscle of appreciation, I gave him an assignment to find something new to appreciate each day and tell a new person why his life was great. It is funny how things change when you value them: they gain in value. In short, they "appreciate." If you don't believe us, try the exercise yourself.

Ground Rules of Appreciation

- Be generous.
- Reflect on what to say.
- Be serious.
- Be specific.
- Take your time.
- [Listener:] Don't respond until the end.

Assignment. Appreciate a colleague or customer or loved one today, and observe the results.

Assignment. Tell at least one person why your life is great.

How did you do? One of the hallmarks of leaders is that they are often the first ones to see what's missing, or to anticipate a problem before anyone else does. After all, this is essential to their ability to lead. But there is also a pitfall: They might forget to recognize what exists already. And one ground rule in life is that if you can stop running after more of what you don't really need, you can make a difference with what you already have. Take Nelson Mandela, who was forced to stop running when he and his ANC comrades were jailed on Robben Island. Instead of becoming bitter about his dire circumstances, he appreciated what his fellow prisoners might bring to the table, and they came up with an ingenious way to make the best of their situation: Each week, another inmate would teach his peers something he knew. Mandela would teach the law; one inmate would be a doctor; one would be a carpenter; and so on.

Day 23: Relationship → Effective Feedback

Date:_______

The truth that's told with bad intent
Beats all the lies you can invent.
William Blake

Imagine you're running a management meeting. How do you keep other managers from being late, goofing off instead of doing their fair share, or dominating the team? What if there's one team member that really riles you? Putting up with him in public but then bashing him privately isn't the answer.

And gossiping about someone who isn't there is understandable—after all, having your friends agree with you is much easier than confronting the culprit—but gossip can destroy teams and even organizations. A key leadership skill is knowing how to give productive feedback. If you have an issue with someone, talk to the person who can do something about it. During your discussion, remind everyone of the group's focus and try to get them back on track.

Feedback is not criticism; feedback is about information. It is the act of describing to another person (with their permission) behaviors that person has that are helpful to you and that you want them to do more of, and/or behaviors that are not helpful that you want the person to do less or not at all.

Do everyone a favor: avoid complaining or make-wrong or, worse, hurling accusations (like "Why do I always end up doing all the work?"). As we saw yesterday, blame and complaints are no-no's—communications that point to the past and only reinforce the very reality you want to change.

Here are the six steps for giving good feedback.

1. Be clear on your intentions before you open your mouth. What do I want us to accomplish? Where do I want us to be at the end of our interaction? And: am I willing to forgive perceived transgressions?
2. Don't barge in. Unless the person is open to your feedback, you're wasting your time. Ask: "Do you have a moment? I'd like to tell you something."
3. Describe specific events. Talk about behaviors, actions, attitudes. Avoid talking about what the person did wrong; instead, talk about your experience. (Distinguish between the facts and your interpretation of the facts.) Avoid characterizations. "You're selfish!" is unlikely to get you what you want.
4. Clarify the consequences of the person's behavior in a personal, self-disclosing statement: "When you don't show up for the mailing, I end up saving the day, but it costs us time for fund raising - and I feel exhausted as a result." Allow yourself to be vulnerable. Above all, no threats here.
5. Ask if the person is open to working out a mutually acceptable solution, and develop a better way together. Explore new possibilities, alternatives. Negotiate an outcome, don't pose an ultimatum. Test your own assumptions: you need to be willing to see where the other person might have different information or see things differently.
6. Thank the person.

Assignment. Take a real issue you have with someone in your life/work. It could be that a colleague of yours does not pull his or her weight sufficiently; that a boss keeps mocking you; or that a direct report is always late with his or her weekly statistics. Apply the feedback process to resolve the issue.

Assignment. Debrief the feedback:

- What did you accomplish / not accomplish?
- What worked / did not work? Which step in the feedback process (see theme 3) did you do especially well, and which not so well?
- What opportunities showed up?
- What's next (both with the issue at hand and with your ability to give productive feedback)?

How did you do? Feedback is one of the most potent tools of leadership. After all, it's precisely what sports coaches do in the locker room during the break or after the game. If you become great at feedback, you can constantly upgrade the game of your people and get them to give their very best.

Day 24: Vision → Basics

Date:_______

All men dream; but not equally...
Those who dream by night in the dusty recesses of their minds
Wake in the day to find that all was vanity;
But the dreamers of the day are dangerous men,
For they may act their dream with open eyes, and make it possible.
T.E. Lawrence

You have now left behind the Relationship level of the Pyramid and can see the peak. This module is about Vision: how can you inspire others to co-create or restore the future? Some have no patience for vision; former German chancellor Helmut Schmidt once famously recommended that visionaries go see an eye doctor. There is nothing wrong with such realists; they are concerned with controlling uncertainty and mastering the physical world. And it is only human to want to reduce the often unbearable tension between the now and the future you want.

The only future-oriented statements so-called realists are willing to make are predictions: "I predict that given our flat performance last year, we will again have one percent growth this year." For them, the future is pretty much an extension of the past. A vision, to deserve the name, should be unpredictable, but still possible to achieve. It should be desirable; it should offer a new quality of life; it should be a magnet for action that gets you out of bed in the morning; it should serve as a strategic filter to weed out irrelevant actions; and it should not be private but be owned by many stakeholders and implementers, just like Nokia's vision above.

The short answer is, you have a future-based conversation. You ask people, "What do you want? Where do you see yourself, or this organization, or this community, or the world in five years from now? What can you not even imagine in your current environment? If you could wave a magic wand, what would you have (or do or be) that you currently don't have (or do or be)? What would you not have (or do or be) that you currently have (or do or be)?"

Ground Rules for Building a Vision

- Make sure the vision is shared. Don't settle for merely persuading them of your vision.People will act powerfully only once they own the vision as theirs.
- Manage the conversation for Vision, or it will deteriorate into mere discussion or opinions.
- Make it safe to speculate, to entertain wild ideas, or to propose seemingly impractical options.
- Do not discuss feasibility until all possibilities have been presented. All possibilities are equally valid.
- Shift conversations that make people right or wrong.

Assignment. As you move to the Vision level of the Pyramid, take stock of your results and accomplishments so far: What was accomplished? What wasn't? What worked? What didn't? What leaders and/or opportunities emerged around you? What's next in delivering your Catalytic Project goals?

Assignment. Have a conversation for vision that creates the future with a co-worker or loved one.

How did you do? Remember: questions usually work better than answers or advice. You don't want to fall into the trap Jürgen Schrempp fell into at the helm of DaimlerChrysler when he sought to impose Daimler's vision onto the joint company. When you co-create a shared vision, the people who co-create it with you will be the visions owners and custodians. Remember the famous quote by the Chinese philosopher Lao Tsu some 2,500 years ago: "When the best leaders' work is done, the people rejoice and say, 'We have done it ourselves.'"

Day 25: Vision → Diagnostics

Date:_______

Where there is no vision,
the people perish.
Proverbs 29:18

How can you see if what's missing in the Pyramid is Vision (as oppposed to, say, Relationship or Strategy)? How do people behave when they lack vision? The warning signs are usually:

- **Extreme risk aversion** (people are very afraid to take risks and try something new);
- **Preoccupation with one's own job** (people are afraid to lose their jobs, or cannot see anything bigger than their own job);
- **Resignation** (people are so locked into the past that they cannot see any new future; everything is "the same as it ever was").

The last one of these is often the most pervasive. Although the job of leaders is to "be today the future that you wish for in the world," as Gandhi put it, managers all too often forget to stand in the future and instead resign themselves to the status quo.

To give just one example: a senior executive at a financial services firm saw in our first coaching session that his *modus operandi* was to find out the rules that others had made for him, and then fit his intentions within those rules, instead of building his own vision and then shaping the rules to match it. The result: "I am too focused on the details; I lose sight of the big picture."

Assignment. In your conversations today, look for signs of Vision being weak or lacking altogether.

How did you do? Sometimes entire societies or cultures can be weak in Vision (for example India in the 1980s). When people say things like, "We tried that last year and it didn't work" or "Here we go again, yet another change effort" or when they are overly concerned with the procedures and lose sight of the big picture, these are surefire signs of a weak Vision level.

Day 26: Vision → Life Commitments

Date:_______

Words do not label things already there.
Words are like the chisel of the carver:
they free the idea, the thing,
from the general formlessness of the outside.
Albert Einstein

Assignment. What are your 7 fundamental life commitments? (Definition: If you don't fulfill a fundamental life commitment, your life is not truly fulfilled. A fundamental life commitment might be to make history, or to build a happy family, or to come up with a path-breaking innovation.)

1.

2.

3.

4.

5.

6.

7.

Once you have articulated your fundamental life commitments, ask yourself:

- How do you currently express each of your fundamental life commitments in action? What are your current projects in behalf of each life commitment?

- Of your 100% resources available (time, money, and relationships), how many percent do you currently allocate to each fundamental life commitment?
- Given your current percent allocation to each fundamental life commitment, what changes do you need to make in your resource allocation in order to meet each commitment?
- What barriers or emergencies (in the areas of 1. finance, 2. communications and relationships, 3. physical environment, and 4. health) is currently holding you back from meeting your fundamental life commitments? Make a checklist and schedule yourself to remove your barriers and/or handle your emergencies.

Assignment. What are your 70 life goals? (Definition: a life goal is anything that comes to mind, without any censorship whatsoever. A life goal might be "I want to see my children getting married," "Go trekking in the Himalayas for a month" or "Own a Jaguar" etc. Tip: Don't stop until you have written down the 70 life goals. It's not important what you write down; the key is to give your imagination free rein and empty your head of all your fantasies.)

1.
2.
3.
4.
5.
6.
7.
8.
9.

10.

11.

12.

13.

14.

15.

16.

17.

18.

19.

20.

21.

22.

23.

24.

25.

26.

27.

28.

29.

30.

31.

32.

33.

34.

35.

36.

37.

38.

39.

40.

41.

42.

43.

44.

45.

46.

47.

48.

49.

50.

51.

52.

53.

54.

55.

56.

57.

58.

59.

60.

61.

62.

63.

64.

65.

66.

67.

68.

69.

70.

How did you do? Make sure that the seven fundamental life commitments span all of your life, including your work, your wealth, your key relationships, and your commitment to society at large. Note that your allocations of time, money, and relationships to the achievement of each fundamental life commitment cannot exceed 100%. My coaching clients often realize that they have poured over 80% of their resources into achieving one or two life commitments, and that the other commitments are lying fallow. That's where the changes come in: What do they want or need to change so that the resource allocations to each commitment are in some balance—or at least allocated by choice?

Day 27: Vision → Economist Article

Date:_______

There are always two parties,
the party of the past and the party of the future;
the establishment and the movement.
Ralph Waldo Emerso

Now that you have some sense of what your life is all about, you have a foundation for designing your 5-year vision. Picture a graph with horizontal bars; the lowest bar is the present, the next higher bar is the future you can predict based on the past and present; a much higher bar is the vision. Note that we are not talking about a dream, which is beyond the vision level (e.g. Martin Luther King's "I have a dream" that one day we will all be brothers) and not attainable. Nor are we talking about what is merely predictable.

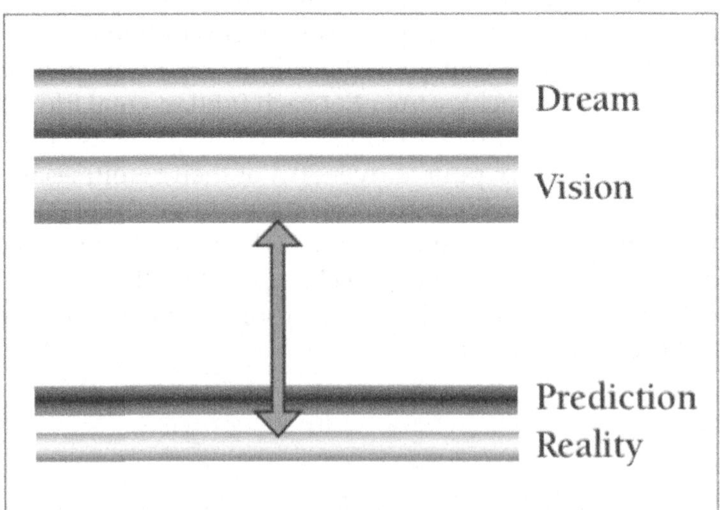

Fig. 5: Vision vs. Prediction vs. Dream

Assignment. Posing as a reporter, write an article about yourself in a well-known business magazine or newspaper (*The Economist*, the *New York Times*, the *Wall Street Journal*, the *Financial Times*, *Der Spiegel* etc.) published on today's date 5 years from now. Be creative and have fun with this.

What changes did you bring about? What difference did you make?

What results did you produce? What did you accomplish? What value did you add for whom?

What was special about your strategy and/or approach?

What did customers say about you? What did VIPs (government officials, captains of industry) say? What did your colleagues (bosses, employees) say?

What did members of your family say?

How do you spend your time on a typical day? What do you do in your spare time?

Once you have written your "5-years-from-now" article, condense the article into a one-sentence 5-year vision of yourself (15 words max):

How did you do? When people distill their 5-year vision article into a concise one-sentence vision, such a statement can serve as a strategic intent, a powerful magnet for action that gets them out of bed in the morning and gives direction and focus to their day-to-day actions. For example, one of my coaching clients crafted this strategic intent: "Create thriving businesses in the technology sector to bring about positive social change and real value for customers and make me financially independent."

Day 28: Vision → Unfinished Business

Date:_______

Be patient towards all that is unresolved in your life,
and try to love the questions themselves. Do not seek the answers
which cannot be given to you because you would not be able to live them,
and the point is to live everything. Live the questions now.
Perhaps you will then gradually, without noticing it,
live some long distant day into the answers.
Rainer Maria Rilke

We carry our pasts around with us like true burdens. Do you know the story about two Buddhist monks who walked from one city to another? They hiked several days, mostly in silence. At one point they came to a river; there was no bridge or ferry in sight. The monks decided to wade through the river where the water was shallow. Suddenly a beautiful young woman appeared. She was too weak to wade through the water by herself and asked the older monk to carry her through the river. He did. The woman slung her slim arms, glistening with sweat, around the old man's neck. He carried her cheerfully across the river and set her down carefully on the opposite bank as the younger monk looked on in amazement. The two monks said good-bye to the girl and continued on their way.

The young monk tried to suppress his agitation as they walked on; but the longer he tried to remain quiet, the more he felt the urge to speak. After several hours, the young monk simply could not hold back anymore. He blurted out, "How could you do this? You know that we are not supposed to touch women. How can you live with this shame?" The older monk smiled serenely and said, "*I* set the woman down hours ago. Of the two of us, which one is still carrying her now?" Like the younger monk, we carry the past with us wherever we go.

A primary role of a leader is to stand for—and in—the future while others are caught in the current circumstances or demands. When obstacles or circumstances get in the way of progress, you often get bogged down in your own history. In order to create new pathways to achieving your original vision, you have to free the present and the future from the shackles of the past. One way to do this is by finishing "unfinished business": unwanted and repetitive patterns (cycles) of behavior that draw their energy from long ago. Here is how you can put the past where it belongs—in the past.

Assignment. List all your unfinished business that drags you back into your past. List items by area:

- Health (e.g. dentist, medical checkup, flossing your teeth);
- Finances (e.g. money owed to you, taxes overdue, money you owe);
- Physical environment (e.g. your closet, clothing, desk, filing cabinet);
- Communications (e.g. unanswered and long overdue mail or email);
- Relationships (e.g. unresolved upset with a colleague, family member or friend).

Schedule by when you will finish each item of unfinished business. (Recommendation: Ask someone else—a colleague or friend or family member whom you can't bear to let down—to be your partner in completing your unfinished business.)

Finish at least one item today.

Debrief: what happened? What did you feel like before, during, and after the completion of the unfinished business item?

How did you do? Many participants in the Leadership-In-Action workshops tackle long-standing items of unfinished business, usually as an overnight assignment. One morning, a participant came in having finally cleared up a tax delinquency that she had avoided for three years; another called his mother after not having spoken to her for almost a decade. The significant energy these leaders had spent on justifying why they hadn't resolved their unfinished business before could now be freed and used for worthier endeavors—and for the future instead of for the past.

Day 29: Vision → Noise vs. Growth

Date:_______

Be willing, at all times, to give up who you are for who you could become.
W.E.B. Du Bois

Assignment. Today, keep a minute-by-minute log of all your activities:

Day/Time	*Area*	*Activity*
Mon/9am-930am	Sales	Strategized sales with direct report
Mon/930am-11am	HR	Interviewed new candidate
Mon/11am-12n	R&D	Met with product development people on bugs in web-based product
Etc.		

Which of these activities do you consider "noise," i.e. you see them as mind-numbing burdens that interrupt and crowd out your inner clarity? List them.

Which of these activities do you consider "growth," i.e. they inspire you, they are on the purpose-line of your life, and they are so compelling that they make you forget dinner? List them.

Given the two lists, what do you need to change (i.e. cancel, delegate etc.)?

How did you do? My coaching clients who do this exercise often discover elements of "growth" within the noise. If you find the weekly staff meeting a tedious bore, you might dig deeper and find that you actually enjoy catching up with certain colleagues and/or getting access to the bigger picture. If you distinguish the boring "noise" aspects of the job (conference calls with the sales team) from the interesting "growth" aspects (strategizing with the CEO), you can minimize or delegate the "noise" aspects. You can then delve further into the "noise" aspects and distinguish more "growth" facets that are actually interesting. You may find that the reporting on the sales calls is boring, while the strategizing of major prospects as a team is downright fascinating. And so on.

Day 30: Vision → Restoring Vision

Date:_______

To believe what has not occurred in history
will not occur at all
is to argue disbelief in the dignity of man.
Gandhi

Perhaps the most important job of a coach is not simply to build vision, but to stand for the future even when others have lost touch with it or have given up altogether. Here are the Six Steps to Restoring Vision:

Step 1: Realize how ever-present resignation is and how easy it is to fall victim to it.
Step 2: Let the person communicate fully and listen with compassion, without intervening or offering quick solutions.
Step 3: Reveal the moment when the person gave up. When exactly did they decide that it couldn't be done? Find out the facts of what happened.
Step 4: Help the person separate what *actually* happened from their *interpretation* of what happened. Put the past where it belongs: into the past.
Step 5: Revisit the person's original vision. Why did they commit to it in the first place?
Step 6: Invite the person to recommit to their vision. If necessary, help them find new pathways.

The **first step** is to recognize how pervasive resignation is. As we have seen on Day 24, resignation is really the result of the past limiting what you believe can happen in the future. An extreme example is Haiti, whose past has left a powerful legacy of defeatism: with thirty-three coups since independence, the world's worst AIDS infection rate outside Africa, and crushing poverty, people are understandably pessimistic. Most Haitians, and with them most people in the international community, believe that things will never change there.

Haiti is only the tip of the iceberg. Resignation lurks everywhere: when we open the morning paper; when we drive to work among countless other cars or in a subway crammed with withdrawn passengers; when we are at work; when we go home and watch TV. Even in teenagers' homes, the background conversation is often, "These are your best years, so shut up and enjoy them." And resignation is oblivious to itself: from the vantage point of resignation, there is no resignation—it looks like realism. "You're dreaming, baby. I know how things are. Believe me, I've been there." Its blindness to itself makes sure that resignation persists. It is the party that has all the votes.

Once you have seen how pervasively the past reigns supreme, the **second step** is to open the lines of communication and simply listen to the person so they can communicate fully where they are. Find out as much as you can about the person and their situation. Look at all aspects of your client's life and, if needed, speak to their family and friends.

Your **third step** is to find out exactly when the person gave up. When did the vision become "impossible," and what was the exact blockage that got in the way? It could be that they missed an interim milestone, or an important gatekeeper dismissed the entire project, or some problem outside of work got in the way. No matter what the interruption was, you want to identify the precise moment, not only to fix problems that may have arisen at that point, but also to hear how the person interprets what occurred. What did they decide? What conclusion did they draw?

Be sure that the person makes a split between the facts and their *perception* of the facts. This is the **fourth step**. In the mid-1980s, when I coached teams in twenty-seven countries to meet their financial objectives, I called a Finnish colleague and asked him how he was doing. There was a long silence on the phone (not untypical for the Fins); I almost thought the line had gone dead. I asked, "Are you there?" Finally he answered in a deep and dark voice, "I think I shall kill myself." All of a sudden I realized: My colleague took his goal so seriously that he would rather die than go on living with the shame of having missed it. His vision had gone out the window. I had to help him see that the facts (he was behind in meeting his financial objectives) were not at all connected to his interpretation (he deserved to die).

Similarly, in Haiti, the calamities of the past have often led to an understandable belief that bad things are bound to happen and that people are victims of circumstances beyond their control: "I can't do anything." It is important to clarify that this is an attitude, not an objective reality.

The **fifth step** is to revisit with the person their original vision; why did they commit to the game in the first place? What would be missing in their life, in their organization, or in their community if they stopped? They may have to step back from the current project or goal, wipe the slate clean, and create their vision again from nothing. One top executive I coached a few years ago saw that he could use his job—a job he had come to see as routine—as an excellent vehicle for fulfilling his own vision, including being a championship performer and yes, making people laugh.

You may have to act as a "wall" for people's commitments so they "kill the alternative," in the words of Margaret Thatcher, of missing the goal. This is the **sixth and final step**. In many ways, the job of a coach is to have a player remember their fundamental commitment when the player forgets. In 1986 I coached a Mexican fundraising team to meet a challenging monthly campaign goal; the end of the month was approaching and they had not been in touch. So I called the team leader and asked how it was going. She said, "They have revoked their goal for the month — they can't see how they can make it." At first I deferred to the team leader; after all, she was senior to me, so who was I to question her conclusion? And I assumed she had already done what she could. But then I followed my intuition and challenged her. I told her it would make a real difference to morale worldwide if the Mexican team led the way, and asked her if they could all recommit to their goal. I don't know what she said to them, but it worked. They recommitted, delivered the goal, and boosted their confidence for all future campaign cycles.

Assignment. Speak with a co-worker or loved one who has lost touch with his or her vision, and help them restore it.

How did you do? My marathon trainer used to say that the running of the marathon is only 10% of the challenge; the other 90% is not physical but mental. So throughout the marathon, you have to manage your mind and its interpretation of what is happening. At mile 20 your mind might tell you, "Stop! What are you doing here? You're out of your mind!" The facts are that your lactic acid has built up, and the tag in the neck of your running shirt is bothering you. Similarly, the fourth step above is a key step: If you can help the other person to draw the distinction between the facts and his/her perception of the facts, that's half the battle. At first they might say, "The management committee is totally against my proposal." Then they might find out that the facts are different: Two management committee members are for the proposal but not speaking up, while three others are skeptical but could be won over.

Day 31: Strategy → Basics

Date:_______

The conventional approach to planning,
with its rigid time frames,
its breakdown of planning tasks into sectors and regions,
and its centralized and technocratic perspective
on plan formulation and implementation
is most unlikely to be effective
in an increasingly turbulent environment.
Francisco R. Sagasti[10]

You have now left behind the Vision level of the Pyramid and are ascending rapidly toward the peak. This module is about Strategy, the bridge between Vision and Action.

Remember that in the context of this WorkBook, Strategy, like all the other levels, is a *conversation* that makes action irresistible, not a thing like a plan or a blueprint that would be too rigid anyway. Static, linear plans are good for building a house or constructing a canalization system in Mumbai, but not for dynamic systems or human organizations.

So at the level of Strategy, in contrast to Vision:

- You should be skeptical, even pessimistic. Ask yourself and others: "What could go wrong?" or "What are the risks?"
- Insist on feasibility until you can see the way through. Insist on evidence that shows the goal is feasible.
- Set clear preferences of some options over others (remember that in Vision all options were equally valid).
- Honor—but don't be bound by—the past.
- Scrutinize the benefits and costs. What will be the budget for the project?

How can you see that Strategy is missing? What are the symptoms? The warning signs are that people are confused or uncertain about what to do; the priorities are unclear and everything seems equally important and/or urgent; there are no specific or measurable goals or milestones; or there is little or no action.

Assignment. As you move from Vision to Strategy, take stock of your Catalytic Project again: What was accomplished / not accomplished? What worked / did not work? What leaders and what opportunities showed up? And what's next given your answers to these questions?

Assignment. In one of your meetings or telephone conversations with co-workers or loved ones today, see if you can reveal the signs of Strategy being weak, insufficient or lacking altogether, and have a conversation that helps them strengthen their Strategy.

How did you do? One colleague of mine was strongly Vision-prone: She was reluctant to think through all of the details of Strategy before taking action. This is a valid way of operating; her vision was crystal-clear, and her actions decisive. But she soon realized that she was wasting valuable energy because she had never asked herself whether her vision was achievable, whether her actions were the high-leverage actions needed, whether the cost-benefit equation was right, whether she had taken the risks and pitfalls into account, or whether her actions were even the right ones. Once the distinction "Strategy" was clear to her, she committed herself to becoming a competent strategist, became a stickler for Strategy, and soon landed the largest consulting deal of her career.

Day 32: Strategy → Strategy-In-Action

Date:_______

Be today the change
that you wish for in the world.
Mahatma Gandhi

Traditional planning is *not* wrong for all purposes. Conventional step-by-step blueprints are well suited for building, say, a bridge, an oilrig, or a new canal system. But in any *living* system, when human dynamics enter the picture, when initiative is needed from all participants, and when planners have to deal with unpredictable variables, conventional planning is woefully inadequate and even counter-productive.

Traditional Planning	**Strategy-In-Action**[11]
• Stable	• Dynamic
• Linear	• Nonlinear
• Strategic and functional fit	• Strategic tension between now and future
• People as objects or recipients	• People as key agents and co-authors
• Focus on structure	• Focus on ideas, perceptions, results
• Cognitive	• Cognitive and intuitive
• Competitive / adversarial	• Competitive / self-improving
• Either / or	• Contextual
• Mechanical	• Organic
• Separating, isolating	• Integrative, comprehensive

Traditional planning is divorced from action. Traditional planning happens in a closed boardroom, the action happens somewhere else, and there is little if any two-way communication between planners and implementers. Planning precedes action and remains static, regardless of the changed landscape caused by those actions.

Traditional planning is top-down, reducing people to recipients or objects of the strategy. Planners expect their fixed blueprint to be realized by the lower echelons. They use buzzwords like "buy-in," but such words reveal that people are at best the buyers, never the co-authors, of the strategy. Top-down planning kills off the most precious asset of organizations in today's knowledge society: the ideas and creativity of all their people.

Traditional planning compartmentalizes organizational functions and ignores both gaps and opportunities. When the left hand doesn't know what the right hand is doing, bottlenecks, failed execution, or massive sunk costs result. One global bank I worked with was riddled with a silo mentality, with each top executive in charge of his or her fiefdom. This led to massive redundancies, since each silo had to have its own infrastructure and staff for doing the exact same things as the other silos.

Traditional planning results in a linear input/output ratio, producing only limited output and failing to exploit the possibilities of nonlinear or high-leverage outputs. In the field of international development, $50 in traditional development assistance produces a $50 hand-pump (assuming no local corruption, and no deduction for administrative expenses for Western development workers who take money to school their children and support their Western lifestyles). This is not inherently wrong, but too slow for producing change on an enormous scale, like the end of hunger.

Traditional planning focuses on expanding a heavy, slow-moving, and costly infrastructure. It sacrifices the ability to turn on a dime and to take entrepreneurial leaps.

Traditional planning attacks isolated problems with a quick-fix approach; it does not reveal the underlying, systemic root causes of problems. And because it does not involve all stakeholders, its solutions are neither comprehensive nor sustainable.

Assignment. In your work/life or in the news, find at least one example each of traditional strategy and of Strategy-In-Action. What are the differences in the approach and in the results?

How did you do? The difference between traditional planning and Strategy-In-Action is far from theoretical; it can be a matter of life and death. Imagine a truck stuck on a road at the Horn of Africa. The truck is full of medical supplies, but it has a flat and cannot move. Another truck drives by; it is empty and could bring all the medicines to the people they are meant for, but since the two trucks belong to two different relief agencies, the empty truck simply drives on without helping. This is no imaginary scenario; it illustrates an all-too-common result of traditional planning.

Day 33: Strategy → Your Strategy-In-Action

Date:_______

There is nothing more difficult to take in hand
or more uncertain in its success
than to take the lead of a new order of things.
Inscription on Niccoló Machiavelli's tomb

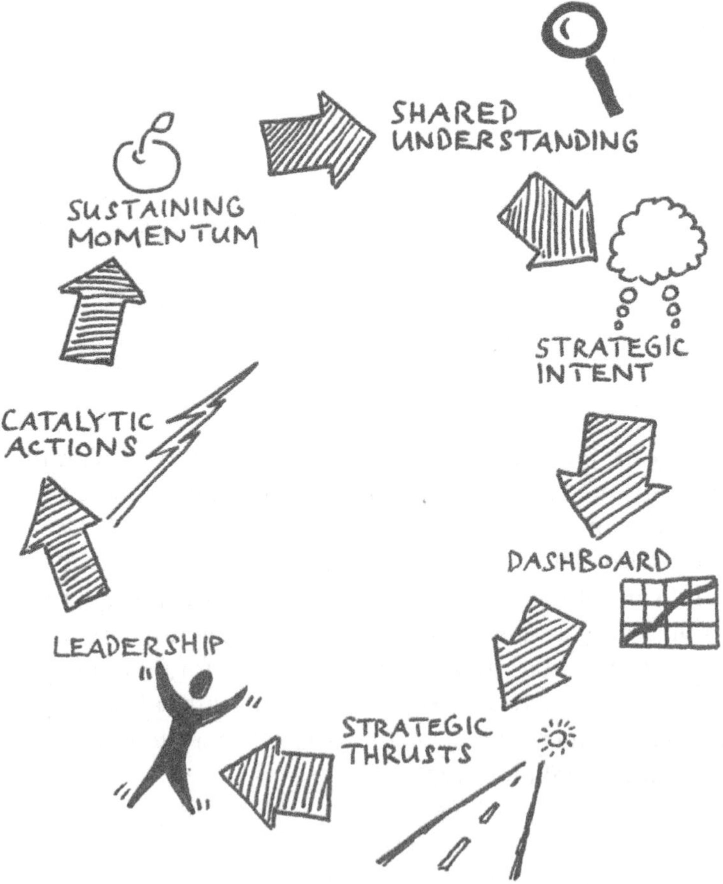

Fig. 6: 7 Steps of Strategy-In-Action

Assignment. Answer the questions below.

1. What is your 5-year strategic intent / vision, i.e. a snapshot of the future that pulls for action; visionary, unpredictable, inclusive, a new quality of life, and measurable?

2. What is currently missing for achieving the strategic intent?

3. What are the current blockages in the way of achieving the strategic intent?

4. What are the current opportunities for achieving the strategic intent?

5. What will be your benchmarks / indicators for achieving the strategic intent?

6. Given your answers so far, what will be the 3-5 key strategic thrusts (drivers) for achieving the strategic intent?

7. Who will be the key leaders (the team) for achieving the strategic intent? What should their roles and accountabilities be?

8. Who will be the key gatekeepers whose support is critical for achieving the strategic intent (and/or who might sabotage or derail the process if they are not aligned)?

9. Who else might be affected (e.g. stakeholders, customers, end-users, beneficiaries)?

10. Given your answers above, what could go wrong? → What are the key success factors for achieving the strategic intent and sustaining the momentum of the process?

How did you do? In working with leaders at 150+ organizations, 30+ of them Fortune 500 companies, I have seen that good people-centered strategy walks a fine line between doing too little and too much planning. Yes, Federal Express grew out of a detailed paper its founder wrote in college; but Microsoft did not. A study of 2,994 startups by the National Federation of Independent Business showed that founders who spent a long time in reflection and planning were no more likely to survive their first three years than people who seized opportunities without planning at all. The above questionnaire aims to walk the middle ground between planning paralysis and no planning at all. You can use it at any level: for your organization's, your department's, or your personal leadership strategy.

Day 34: Strategy → Cross-Cultural Strategy

Date:_______

We aren't passengers on Spaceship Earth, we're the crew.
We aren't residents on this planet, we're citizens.
The difference in both cases is responsibility.
Astronaut Rusty Schweikert

Today we focus on cross-cultural strategy. We have already seen at the Self-Awareness level (on Day 12) how you avoid costly culture clashes by decoding other cultures (organizational or geographical). But how can you be a cross-cultural strategist, capitalize on globalization, and manage effectively across borders? Cross-cultural savvy is not merely a self-management or HR skill; it is a strategic skillset. Unfortunately many multinationals fail to harvest the most precious resources—ideas and innovation—from the far-flung regions in which they operate. And they suffer for it.

Meet Yves Doz, professor of global technology and innovation at the international business school INSEAD, France, who posits a new type of global corporation attuned to the dynamics of the knowledge economy: the "metanational." Doz describes the metanational as "a company that builds a new kind of competitive advantage by discovering, accessing, mobilizing, and leveraging knowledge from many locations around the world."

Becoming a global company once meant penetrating markets around the world. A traditional multinational develops a standard product for its home market, and then sells or "projects" that standard around the world. But the demands of the knowledge economy are turning this strategy on its head. Today, the challenge is to innovate by *learning from the world.* And because innovation drives growth, those companies that fail to learn will be left behind.

Doz and his colleagues define the metanational by three core capabilities:

- Being the first to identify and capture new knowledge emerging all over the world
- Mobilizing this globally scattered knowledge to out-innovate competitors
- Turning this innovation into value by producing, marketing, and delivering efficiently on a global scale

Managers can build a metanational advantage for their own organizations in several ways, including:

- Prospecting for and accessing untapped pockets of technology and emerging consumer trends from around the world.
- Leveraging knowledge imprisoned in the multinational's local subsidiaries.
- Mobilizing this fragmented knowledge to generate innovations, profits, and shareholder value.

Although he singles out no one company as a perfect metanational, Doz identifies hotspots of learning capability in such innovators as Nokia, in cell phones; Shiseido Company Ltd., in perfumes; and STMicroelectronics NV, in semiconductors. He notes that each of these companies benefited from "being born in the wrong place," that is, outside the recognized centers of critical knowledge for their industries, and so had no choice but to learn from world markets.

Even the U.S. armed forces have learned that lesson. A few days after 9/11, I received a call from the U.S. Military Academy at West Point. The colonel on the phone, the head of West Point's leadership program, said curtly, "Tom, we need you over here." It turned out that the highest brass of the U.S. Army had realized that military officers needed to be trained not only as competent fighters, but also as skillful and empathetic diplomats. This was not a question of being nice to terrorists; it was a strategic question of decoding how they ticked in order to anticipate their moves. The Army knew what many companies don't: empathy is not merely a nice-to-have HR skill—it is a strategic competence. When I helped West Point integrate intercultural skills into its curriculum, the assembled faculty asked me how the cadets could put themselves in the shoes of militant Islamists. I pointed out to the faculty that to truly know Al Qaeda, its culture and ways of thinking, cadets needed to study things like the Koran and the history of Islam. Now all courses at West Point have a cross-cultural component.

If this is true for defense, it is just as true in business competition; to anticipate Google's moves, Microsoft or I.B.M. strategists must put themselves in Google's shoes.

Assignment. Take an action that allows you to learn best practices, or a feature of innovation, from another culture (either within your company or from a contact in your sphere of influence). For example, contact a colleague in a remote location, or in another department, and interview that colleague about his/her practices, or ask him/her for an idea of how you or the organization could do things differently.

How did you do? Why do senior managers at headquarters seldom push for path-breaking innovation? Because they are the ones who benefit the most from the status quo, so they also have the most to lose from change. People in the periphery, in remote locations, might have the radical new ideas the company needs to take an entrepreneurial leap.

Day 35: Strategy → Global Meetings

Date:_______

I am a citizen,
not of Athens or Greece,
but of the world.
Socrates

Swiss, and later American, pharmaceutical companies started using teamwork in the 1950s to develop new prescription drugs. Team members included medical experts and people from production, finance, legal and patents, and marketing. More recently, the Internet and outsourcing activities have led to "virtual teams" whose members are working together remotely—from home or in different parts of the country or world.

C.K. Prahalad and Kenneth Lieberthal have argued that as of 2010, thirty to forty percent of top teams at multinationals no longer come from the United States or Europe, but from the largest emerging markets—especially China, India, and Brazil. This means that top managers can no longer assume that their usual jokes or sports references will be understood by their peers.

How can you create, lead, influence and debrief meetings effectively when the people on your team have different cultural backgrounds and/or are spread out in different parts of the country or the world? (By "effectively" I mean that the meetings produce the results you want, that they enable co-creation, and that they result in alignment among the participants and the experience of partnership and team.)

Before: Co-Create the Agenda.

- Any meeting, whether live or virtual, is only as good as its preparation. You will have the (video) conference that you prepare for and for which you prepare every participant. If you want to cause a breakthrough at a meeting, you had better cause that breakthrough in the minds of a critical mass of participants beforehand.
- See the meeting as a step in a process. Look at it not as an isolated event, but as an integral part of your company strategy for unleashing leadership.
- Stand in the shoes of every participant. What are people's intentions, what are their concerns, what are their dreams? Stand in their shoes and see the world from their perspective. What might be important to Jim right now? What matters most to the Mexicans?
- Co-create the purpose, intended results, and agenda of the meeting. As much as possible, design the meeting with the people who will be participating. It works when you send a draft agenda to all participants before the meeting happens (make sure to call it a draft, so they don't feel it is cast in stone). It works when they know the agenda beforehand. And it works when you ask participants what they think about the agenda.
- Pay attention to local time zones and local customs of the participants. Schedule the meeting time so that it occurs during work hours for all the participants - or at least so that it's not in the middle of the night in Melbourne or on a national holiday in Venezuela.

During: Keep Things on Track.

- When you open the meeting, say, "Good morning, good afternoon, and good evening," or whatever the appropriate welcome would be given the locations of the participants. Also be aware of what season it is in the parts of the world where your participants are. A global teleconference can easily include New Yorkers who have battled a snowstorm to get to work and

Argentineans who are leaving on their summer vacation the next weekend. Paying attention to such details will have the participants be more real for you, and you to them.

- Lead from the big picture, from your vision. Don't let details get in the way of accomplishing your purpose and intended results. Human beings seem to be wired to be distracted by the operational details. If an operational issue shows up during the meeting, get it handled off-line or create a task force to deal with it after the meeting.
- Speak and listen to every person as *the* key to the meeting. Whether it is the company's president or its receptionist, that person is the key to the success of the conference. So treat each and every person in the meeting that way.
- It helps to use a dose of British understatement and self-deprecating humor when you address a global audience—to show them that you are not too full of yourself. One example of this is Tim Melville-Ross, the former head of the Institute of Directors, a British organization of individual company directors. He opened his speech to the institute's 1998 annual convention with these words:

> It is a real pleasure to speak to such a large and distinguished audience. If you will forgive me just a moment's conceit, it at least shows that in this respect my career has not been without progress. The first ever speech I made was in a village hall on a filthy February evening. It was cold, the wind was blowing, the snow was falling and there was just one other person present. I felt I owed it to the fellow to go ahead, so I made my speech and he applauded politely and I left the platform, put on my coat and was about to depart when I felt a hand on my

> shoulder. He said to me: "Please don't go—I'm the next speaker!" Thank you all for being here.

After: Leverage the Momentum.

- Complete the meeting by acknowledging everyone who made a key contribution to its success, including the hosts, the agenda team, the presenters, the production team, and the people who produced materials.
- Debrief the meeting, both alone and with your agenda team. Ask these questions:
  1. Did we accomplish the purpose of the meeting?
  2. Which intended results did we achieve, and which not (and what is next in achieving the results we missed)?
  3. What worked and should be done again in the future, and what did not work and should be avoided?
  4. What promises and requests were made at the meeting, and who needs to be reminded or followed up with?
  5. What, if anything, is incomplete for any of the participants?
  6. What about the meeting should be communicated to people who did not attend - how can they be empowered with the results or shared understanding of the meeting?
  7. And finally, what is next to keep up the momentum from the meeting?

Assignment. Design, produce, lead and debrief your own cross-cultural meeting, teleconference or videoconference (virtual or in-person) that is necessary for your 100-Day Catalytic Project to succeed, and in which you mobilize at least five participants to produce a specific intended outcome. If you don't do business across national borders, you might hold a cross-cultural meeting across racial, ethnic, or cultural borders within your own community or country.

Debrief: What did you accomplish? What did you not accomplish? What worked (before, during, and after the meeting)? What did not work? Write the debrief in bullet format below.

How did you do? I was once a fly on the wall during a weekly teleconference a company president held with the top managers of the European subsidiaries. It was painful to be there: mechanical, perfunctory, linear, boring, and no fun at all. The president simply went around and asked each manager to report. The climate was full of fear, which did not exactly lead to lots of creativity. There was no appreciation, no humanity, no co-creation. When you facilitate a teleconference, think of yourself as a composer and conductor of great music. Your job is to have each participant be a virtuoso who contributes to the symphony.

Day 36: Action → Basics

Date:_______

Whatever you can do or dream you can, begin it.
Boldness has genius, power and magic in it.
Begin it now.
Johann Wolfgang von Goethe

Congratulations! You have climbed from Self-Awareness to Relationship, and then from Vision to Strategy; now you can scale the pinnacle of the Global Leader Pyramid®: Action, where you have powerful conversations that mobilize others for results. (Remember, Action in the context of the Pyramid is not a thing but a set of effective conversations.)

How do you know that you need to work on the Action level? It's simple: You know when you lack decisive actions or results; or when people don't keep their agreements. (Note that if people don't do what they said they would, you often have to go back to a lower level of the Pyramid and do more work on the Self-Awareness, Relationship, Vision, or Strategy levels. In those cases, the lack of actions or results is merely a symptom of weak lower levels of the Pyramid.)

At the Action level of any project, you might ask, "Who will do what by when?" The idea of conversations for action is that you speak not *about* the action, merely representing the action, but you speak the action itself.

For example, if I say, "I love you" and mean it, I am not speaking *about* love, but the love is conveyed through my very words. This is what the German philosopher Martin Heidegger meant when he said that "Language is the house of being": Language has the power to convey not just words, but the essence of what it bespeaks.

There are several pitfalls in conversations for action that you should be aware of:

- Not expressing your expectations fully and clearly; leaving things vague and not making crystal clear what you want and by when.
- Not specifying who will be accountable for the action, and by when the action will be taken.
- Asking for a behavior change rather than asking for an action (e.g., asking your direct report to be a better manager is not a true request; asking him or her to evaluate three business prospects this week is).
- Slipping into unproductive forms of speech (rumors, excuses, blame, ultimatums; see Day 20 on Speaking)
- Penalizing others for declining requests or revoking their promises.
- Not taking your—or other people's—words seriously.

Assignment. Now that you are ready to scale the Action level, assess your progress so far. What was accomplished / not accomplished? What worked / didn't work? What leaders / opportunities emerged? And out of all this, what is next?

Assignment. Observe your conversations with your colleagues. When are you (or they) slipping from conversations for Action into non-productive forms of speech, for example justifying non-performance, explaining the past, blaming the circumstances, giving your opinion without responsibility, or passing the buck to someone else?

How did you do? In my work with leaders and their organizations over the last 25 years, one thing struck me over and over: How much time managers spend in conversations that are not designed to elicit Action. It is very hard to measure the cost of such useless chatter, but the waste must be in the billions of dollars for lost productivity each year. To illustrate: If 1,000 people work for a company, each making an average of $30 per hour, and they spend one hour a day babbling at the copier or water cooler, the company loses $62 million a year.

Day 37: Action → On Accomplishment

Date:_______

We are still far from pondering
the essence of action decisively enough.
We view action only as causing an effect.
The actuality of the effect is valued according to its utility.
But the essence of action is accomplishment.
To accomplish means to unfold something
into the fullness of its essence,
to lead it forth into this fullness.
Martin Heidegger

Toyota offers free, in-depth tours of its US-operations, including product development and distributor relations, to anyone, even to its competitors. Why? Because visitors cannot copy Toyota's true advantage—the way it executes or carries out its strategy.[12] Toyota is adept at accomplishment.

You can create a vision, design a strategy, and establish and empower a body of leadership, but until you have accomplishment, you are not truly a leader. Accomplishment is Vision and Strategy made real. It is richer than mere results. A result does not require volition; an accomplishment does. Driving into a tree after skidding on a patch of ice is a result. You do not have to want to hit the tree in order to crash into it. In fact, you probably try to avoid it. In contrast, a marathon is an accomplishment that requires enormous willpower and sustained commitment. Accomplishment is the achievement of Vision. It is deliberate success, manifest intention, Strategy implemented, Vision expressed in results.

Yet accomplishment is perhaps the most elusive component of leadership. As a society, we have not yet decoded what it takes to accomplish—"to unfold something into the fullness of its essence," as Martin Heidegger put it in the quote above. CEOs get excessive pay packages that are not tied to performance. Entrepreneurs rush to IPOs without building profitability. Shareholders expect instant gratification. Politicians make promises to voters, but fail to keep them once elected. International conferences make ambitious resolutions, but follow-up gets mired in red tape.

Most of us can see the lack of accomplishment in our day-to-day lives. Either we are so busy that we have no room to step back and think strategically, or we dream of the future without considering the actions we need to take today to make that future real. How often do you find yourself doing things that have nothing to do with your purpose? How often do you allow your intentions to be thwarted by demands, e-mails, and paperwork that merely add to the aimless busy-ness that runs your life? We are no closer to accomplishment when we dream without making our dreams come true. How often have you heard yourself say, "I want to lose ten pounds," "I'd love to travel," "I've always wanted to be an entrepreneur," or some other New Year's resolution on which you never followed through?

Assignment. Take 3-5 recent results in your life and/or work. See if you can express these outcomes in the language of true accomplishments.

How did you do? The trick is that accomplishment lives in language: You can take a result and express that result in the language of accomplishment. In other words, accomplishment is something you stand for, by declaration. A colleague of mine recently closed a large deal with a new client for a Coaching-In-Action engagement. That's a result. The accomplishment she can stand for and declare? "This is the largest contract I ever closed; it puts my consulting into sustainable viability."

Day 38: Action → Speech Acts

Date:_______

Words have come to be very cheap,
particularly in our circles.
They ceased to be commitments.
Gone is the sensitivity to their power.
Abraham J. Heschel

Some forms of speech are more suited to be effective conversations for Action than others.

Basic Moves in a Conversation for Action	
Request—specific actions / results in a specific time frame.	"I ask that you do (x) by (time y). "I ask that you give me the report by end of business Friday."
Invitation—non-specific	"Would you like to have lunch with me today?" "You might want to take on that marketing job."
Offer—non-specific	"What if I pay for lunch next time?"
Possible Responses:	
Promise—specific actions / results in a specific time frame.	"I accept your request; I will do it." (When you accept the request, you are committed.) "I will give you that report by end of business Friday."
Counter-Offer	"Yes - as long as we agree on some changes."
Promise a Committed Response Later	"I promise I'll get back to you about this by _____." You promise to have the conversation and give them a commitment (accept, decline or counter-offer) at a later time that you specify.
Decline	"No. I can't or won't do this." Declining a request means that you commit not to do some

	work. This commitment leaves the customer free to seek another performer.
Request for Clarification	"Can you tell me more about this?"

The crucial thing about all these types of conversations for Action is that they entail the freedom to accept, to decline, to counter-offer, or to promise a response at a specific later time. This freedom is in contrast to command-and-control forms of speech like orders, demands, or instructions where the receiver has no choice but to accept, and where the implied subtext is often, "If you don't do what I told you to do, your career will suffer—if you don't get fired first." The freedom to accept, decline or counter-offer lies at the heart of the co-leader approach.

Assignment. Make 2-3 powerful promises and 2-3 powerful requests to/of people around you who are involved in your 100-Day Catalytic Project.

How did you do? In my work with all types of organizations, it's striking how rarely people use the language of Action above. They say all kinds of things, except promises or requests with measurable deliverables and clear deadlines that would move the Action forward. Recently a colleague pointed out to me that my website was not sufficiently search-optimized. I asked her, "Do you have a promise or a request?" She immediately realized that she had presented a problem not a solution; and she formulated a clear request not of me, but of the web designer. It took us two minutes to move from problem to Action, and the exercise averted a lot of useless and costly spinning of wheels.

Day 39: Action → 4 Pitfalls With Bad News

Date:_______

Perhaps all the dragons in our lives are princesses
who are only waiting to see us act,
just once, with beauty and courage.
Rainer Maria Rilke

A captain of industry was once asked, "How did you become chairman?" He answered with his usual brevity: "Two words: right decisions." The questioner insisted, "But how did you learn to make the right decisions?" The chairman's retort was again concise: "One word: experience." "But how did you get experience?" "Two words," the chairman shot back. "Wrong decisions."

The chairman had a good grasp of the link between mistakes and successes—like Winston Churchill who used to say that "Success is going from failure to failure without loss of enthusiasm." But most of us have a less playful attitude toward breakdowns; we tend to fall into four typical traps when the going gets tough. While these pitfalls are only human and perfectly understandable, each of them is counter-productive.

Pitfall #1: Shame. One pitfall is that—because you see the breakdown as something negative, even shameful—you keep it a secret. When we see breakdowns as bad, we tend to react badly. We feel stressed. We get upset. We panic. Whether it is trouble with a co-worker or being behind on a deadline, our instinct is to try to keep breakdowns secret and fix them before others might find out (or do nothing at all and hope someone else will fix them - but more about that below).

Most of us live in a culture that shuns failure. We want to avoid bombing out or giving bad news to superiors or colleagues. We want to have it all figured out before (or if ever) we go public.

But the costs of keeping breakdowns secret can be huge. In the mid-1980s Xerox executives had a rude awakening when a major new product, the 5046 mid-range copier, failed in the market because of serious reliability problems. How could this happen, given the company's focus on Leadership Through Quality (LTQ), a quality-assurance process set up by the then-CEO David Kearns? After investigating, Kearns found that Xerox managers at all levels were aware of the problems but they had conspired to keep it quiet. The cover-up had extended to the highest levels of management; but for this code of silence, the faulty copier would have never been introduced. What particularly distressed Kearns was that Xerox had set up the LTQ process precisely to prevent a similar fiasco. But the process had failed because "the old culture of our people being afraid to deliver bad news was not yet rinsed from the company."[13] In all fairness, Kearns was not entirely innocent; some said he had failed to eliminate multiple management layers and to institutionalize a culture of full communication throughout the company. This twin problem had an unintended outcome: crucial information never reached top management. Be that as it may; the fact is that managers did not make the copier breakdown public, and it cost them their jobs and jeopardized Xerox's reputation and bottom line.

Pitfall #2: Blame. Unforeseen breakdowns, or dragons as the poet Rainer Maria Rilke called them, are inevitable stations on the leader's journey. But they can make you want to rip out your hair, chew your nails, or yell in uncontrollable rage at everyone around you. Though a leader's ultimate test is how he or she copes in a crisis, the smartest CEOs have been known to regress and throw temper tantrums when the world seemed to turn against them.

Jeffrey Skilling, the disgraced former CEO of Enron, was so famous for his tongue-lashings that employees simply were too afraid to come up and say the truth to him. Even alarm-ringer Sherron Watkins chose to express her concerns anonymously instead of coming right out with them. And she was one of the brave ones. But unfortunately Enron is far from alone—despite a decade of shareholder activism. "I was never allowed to present to the board unless things were perfect," said a former Xerox executive. "You could only go in with good news." Whoever gave the bad news ran the risk of being blamed or fired: the board would simply kill the messenger. And when directors forced executives to confront their poor results, executives repeatedly blamed them on short-term factors—from currency fluctuations to trouble in Latin America. By the time then-president (and soon CEO) Anne Mulcahy came out and spoke the truth—the company had an "unsustainable business model," she told analysts in 2000—Xerox was already flirting with bankruptcy.

This is the second pitfall when breakdowns happen: you cast blame on yourself, on your colleagues, or on the game as a whole—"*I* am wrong, *they* are wrong, or *it* is wrong." (The "it" may be the task, the project, your job, or the entire organization.)

Pitfall #3: Hope. The third pitfall is that you simply wait, hoping that the breakdown will somehow disappear "if we just let it be." It probably won't. But often nothing happens, especially in organizations where people tend to pass the buck, unless someone—a leader—takes charge and cuts through the apathy.

A *Fortune* magazine survey of failed CEOs found a surprising commonality among them: they tend to wait instead of facing a breakdown head-on. "What is striking, as many CEOs told us, is that they usually know there's a problem; their inner voice is telling them, but they suppress it. Those around the CEO often recognize the problem first, but he isn't seeking information from multiple sources."[14] Worse, when CEOs feel threatened, "they focus even more on what brought them their success," says leadership expert Warren Bennis, a professor at the Marshall School of Business, University of Southern California. "They dismiss anything that clashes with their beliefs." Such attachment to old solutions is, of course, the exact opposite of what would help them transform the breakdown into a breakthrough.

Pitfall #4: Hedge. Finally, and perhaps worst of all, you change (and usually lower) your background commitment instead of stretching to fill the gap. But the commitment is not the problem. Quite the opposite: it is the solution. Whenever you have a commitment, you are bound to have a gap between your current situation and your vision; breakdowns come with the territory. In fact, breakdowns cannot exist without background commitments. If you are not committed to anything, you may have problems (you might turn into a vegetable, you atrophy, you become dull), but you will not have breakdowns (or accomplishments) of size.

Assignment. Take a close look at a recent breakdown in your enterprise. How did you and/or your colleagues fall victim to one or several of the four pitfalls of shame, blame, hope or hedge?

How did you do? A coaching client of mine confessed that "my emotional reaction to breakdowns is in and of itself a breakdown." He is not alone. When things don't go according to plan, it's only human to react with feelings boiling over. As we will see tomorrow, there is a way to be senior to those emotions and to make the lemons on your path into lemonade. The key is to recognize that breakdowns, far from being bad, are the essential ingredient for breakthroughs.

Day 40: Action → A New View of Failure

Date:_______

It is not the critic who counts;
not the man who points out how the strong man stumbled
or where the doer of deeds could have done them better.
The credit belongs to the man who is actually in the arena,
whose face is marred with dust and sweat and blood;
who strives valiantly; who errs and comes short again and again;
who knows the great enthusiasms, the great devotion;
who spends himself in a worthy cause;
who, at the best, knows the triumph of high achievement,
and at the worst, at least fails while daring greatly.
Theodore Roosevelt

To avoid the four pitfalls of shame, blame, hope, and hedge from yesterday, we need a new view of *failure*. At first glance, failure is bad and must be avoided at all costs. Effective leaders use a much different interpretation: they see—and harness—breakdowns not as problems but as opportunities, as raw material for accomplishment. If you take the negativity out, a breakdown is simply a gap between the present and the future you want. *Breakdowns are necessary for breakthroughs in productivity.*[15]

A study of thirteen significant commercial advances in sixteen companies from 1966 to 1986 found that the one thing common to all of them was a leader's obsessive urge to solve "a problem." Groundbreaking innovations common today, from the VCR to the CAT scanner, from Nautilus machines to Fed-Ex, from Nike to Club Med, arose like Phoenixes from the ashes of breakdowns when they were originally conceived.

Perhaps the classic example of a breakthrough resulting from a breakdown was the Post-It revolution. It all began when Spence Silver, an inventor at 3M, discovered in 1968 that he had accidentally invented glue that was more tacky than adhesive. Silver visited every single division of 3M, but could not find anybody who could make use of his strange invention. In fact he had to wage a battle even to get his new glue patented, which 3M did only with great reluctance. It was not until 1974, six years later, that Art Fry, a colleague of Silver's, accidentally dropped his hymn book to the floor, and all the paper slips he had used to mark the pages fluttered out. It was at that moment that Fry had his "Eureka!" moment. If Silver had given up or not seized this breakdown as his opportunity for a breakthrough, the Post-It would not have seen the light of day, and would have never become the blockbuster business it is for 3M.[16]

Earlier innovations too were the result of a leader who embraced breakdowns as opportunities. Take Thomas Edison, without whom we might all still use candles to read at night. Did you know that it took Edison some one thousand attempts before he finally invented the electric light bulb? His contemporaries kept ridiculing him, and even his supporters counseled him to give up on his hopeless quest. The story goes that one young reporter came to interview him and asked him outright, "Mr. Edison, why do you persevere with this endeavor, after failing five hundred times to make it work?" Edison replied, "Young man, you have got it all wrong. I haven't failed five hundred times. I have simply discovered five hundred ways of how not to make an electric light bulb." Edison celebrated each time a trial did *not* work; he stubbornly insisted that each failed trial brought him one step closer to the trial that would work. He was right, and we owe electricity to his tenacity, his dedication to his vision, and his love of failures.

Take one more recent example: when Pfizer sought to develop a new heart medicine, trial tests of the drug Sildenafil in 1994 showed unwelcome and huge (forgive the pun) side-effects: male patients who took the drug experienced increased blood flow to the penis. The drug acted by enhancing the smooth muscle relaxant effects of nitric oxide, a chemical that is normally released in response to sexual stimulation. If Pfizer managers had been ashamed, if they had conspired to keep the malfunctions a secret, if they had done nothing and waited, or if they had lowered the bar on their commitment to make a blockbuster drug, nothing would have happened: they would have preserved the status quo and lost the company a lot of R&D money. But they made noise, and to make a long story short, out of a breakdown—a malfunctioning heart drug—a breakthrough was born. The new drug posted $1 billion in sales in its first year and became a household name: Viagra.

Assignment. Fail intentionally once or twice (ideally in conjunction with your 100-Day Catalytic Project). Each time, take on something of which you know that you will fail. Debrief: what happened? What are your observations out of this exercise?

How did you do? Failing intentionally is not an easy thing; but unless you are willing to fail, it will be tough for you to grow. For example, I am a reasonably competent breaststroke swimmer, but have always avoided the crawl. In 2009 I seized the chance to take a crawling course at the local public pool. I looked really stupid, felt like I drank most of the water in that pool, and nearly drowned several times, but taking on a domain of obvious incompetence was exhilarating. By now you know my fondness for quotes; here is another one by Teddy Roosevelt. "Far better it is to dare mighty things, to win glorious triumphs, even though checkered by failure, than to take rank with those poor spirits who neither enjoy much nor suffer much, because they live in the gray twilight that knows not victory nor defeat."

Day 41: Action → Declaring a Breakdown

Date:_______

Our greatest glory lies not in never falling
but in rising every time we fall.
Ralph Waldo Emerson

How can you turn adversity into advantage in day-to-day management? Say your goal is to generate $2.5 million in sales this year and you are at $800,000 in July. You can keep this shortfall quiet, blame others, wait for something to happen, or lower the goal; *or* you can take the leadership route of declaring a breakdown. You can make change by following the simple sequence below.

3-Step Breakdown-to-Breakthrough Process

Step 1: Declare a breakdown and make it public until everyone confronts the breakdown.

Step 2: Assert your background commitment. (There would be no breakdown without a commitment in the background.)

Step 3: Search for new options and pathways to your background commitment; declare the breakthrough.

Step 1: Declare a Breakdown. The first step is to make the breakdown public in a way that interrupts business-as-usual. Make the gap highly visible. Tell others about it. Your declaration of the breakdown forces you and your colleagues to confront the gap between current and desired performance. A breakdown in this context is not a thing; it is a declaration, a speech act that puts you back in the driver's seat.

Some leaders declare breakdowns non-verbally; actions speak louder than words. On Thursday evening, December 1, 1955, after a long day as a seamstress in a Montgomery, Alabama department store, Rosa Parks took the bus home. When all the seats reserved for "colored" people in the back were taken, she, along with three other African-American riders, decided to do the unthinkable: she sat down on a whites-only seat. She got a few furtive glances from other passengers, white and black, but nothing happened. In an interview many years later, she told what happened next: "We were not disturbed until we reached the third stop after I boarded the bus. At this point a few white people boarded the bus, and one white man was left standing. When the driver noticed him standing, he spoke to us (the man and two women across the aisle) and told us to let the man have the seat. The other three all stood up."

But Parks had finally had enough of being treated as a second-class citizen. As a "Negro," she had put up with unequal treatment on city buses, as well as in stores, restaurants, movie theaters, and other places for years. She was tired of it - and somehow, on this cold winter evening, something within her shifted. It was as if a switch had been thrown. Parks decided she was not going to take it anymore. "The driver saw me still sitting there. He said would I stand up, and I said, 'No, I will not.'" The driver kept shouting at her to move; she simply kept saying no. The angry bus driver put on the emergency brake, got out of his seat, and marched over to Mrs. Parks. He demanded that she move to the back of the bus; she still refused to get up. "Then he said, 'I'll have you arrested.' And I told him he could do that." He left the bus and returned with a policeman. Parks was promptly arrested for violating segregation laws.

Instead of saying much, Rosa Parks just sat there. But her simple action was one of the most effective declarations of a breakdown in history. Her sitting there quietly amounted to an outcry over the gap between a status quo of accepted but unacceptable racial discrimination and a possible future of racial equality and respect. She was unwilling to tolerate any longer what society had condoned for too long, and she was willing to go all the way. "Usually, if I have to face something, I do so no matter what the consequences might be. I never had any desire to give up. I did not feel that giving up would be a way to become a free person."[17]

In your own life and work, what has become unacceptable once you think about it? Perhaps it is the insufficient partnership with a direct report or your boss, or the current slow turnaround from sales to delivery and invoicing, or a new product's overblown development costs. Perhaps you are not satisfied with the way you listen to colleagues or family members, the way the CEO listens to you, or the permission you have to challenge the head of a subsidiary. These breakdowns are not bad in and of themselves; by declaring them as insufficient, you put them under the microscope and make clear your intent to move to higher level—from good to great, or from great to extraordinary. In short, you can use breakdowns as tools for quality assurance.

In our example of the $2.5 million sales breakdown, you may have to be a bit impertinent. Put up a big flipchart right at the office entrance and write in bold letters:

I DON'T CARE WHAT YOU THINK OF ME, BUT - ON OUR TARGET OF $2.5 MILLION WE ARE AT $800,000 AND IT'S JULY. WHAT ARE WE GOING TO DO ABOUT IT?

Assignment. Declare a breakdown around you, either in your 100-Day Catalytic Project or elsewhere in your work/life. Declare the breakdown to those people who can do something about it.

How did you do? Remember: breakdowns are not bad; they are not problems to solve; they are simply opportunities to transform areas in your work or life that have become unacceptable. In that way, they are tools for quality assurance.

Day 42: Action → Background Commitment

Date:_______

Seek, above all, for a game worth playing.
Such is the advice of the oracle to modern man.
Having found the game, play it with intensity –
play as if your life and sanity depended on it.
Follow the example of the French existentialists and flourish a banner bearing the word 'engagement.'
Robert S. Deropp

Step 2: Assert your Background Commitment. The second step in turning adversity into advantage is to keep in mind your underlying goal, without which there would be no gap. By declaring the breakdown, you serve public notice that something is unacceptable *in relation to a particular commitment.* This is far from an act of resignation or defeatism—quite the opposite. To declare a gap requires vision and commitment. By declaring it, you shine a harsh light on something that you say is unsatisfactory. Just like in the example of Churchill's warnings against Hitler, others might not see it as a problem. It might not even be inherently bad; but relative to your commitment it shows up as insufficient. In our example, current sales by themselves are not a problem; they are just that, current sales. They are insufficient only against the background of your intention to produce $2.5 million. Remember, and help others remember, why everyone committed to the goal in the first place. Revisit the original vision; why did you and your team choose this game? What would be missing in your lives, in your organization, or in society if you stopped?

Assignment. Take the breakdown you declared yesterday, and revisit your commitment or vision in the background. What are you committed to that makes the current situation show up as a breakdown?

How did you do? Instead of butting your head against the same wall over and over again, step back and see what commitment in the background gave rise to the current breakdown. Once a leader is clear on his/her background commitment, he/she can often find new pathways to the goal and leap over the wall.

Day 43: Action → Options for the Breakthrough

Date:_______

Security is mostly a superstition.
It does not exist in nature,
nor do the children of men as a whole experience it.
Avoiding danger is no safer in the long run
than outright exposure.
Life is either a daring adventure, or nothing.
Helen Keller

Step 3: Search for Options and declare the Breakthrough. The third step is to call a meeting or videoconference with all relevant stakeholders, and brainstorm extraordinary actions that will fill the gap. Don't be afraid to wake people up and rattle them enough so they shift their focus, do new thinking, and see opportunities they didn't consider before. Once you have declared the breakdown and have recommitted yourself and your team to the original goal, do a brainstorming. Explore innovative options and catalyze uncommon actions in order to fill the gap between the status quo and the desired result.

Consider:

- If you don't change anything, where will you likely end the year (for example $1.5 million in sales instead of your $2 million goal)?
- If you were on-target to meet your goal, what would the desired performance level look like right now—in July and August?
- What new pathways could you take to get there?
- What resources have you not even considered yet?
- What options are still untapped?
- What in this breakdown is an opportunity in disguise?

Be sure to step back from your fixation on old pathways or solutions that may have worked in the past but are used up or too limited now—in James Weick's words, be sure to "drop your tools."

Jack Welch defined leadership as "looking reality straight in the eye and then acting upon it with as much speed as you can." Sounds simple, but few people have the guts to do it; and you cannot possibly take on every problem in your environment. So choose your battles carefully: be strategic in what breakdowns you declare and strive to turn into breakthroughs. No matter what you do, remember this: a true leader sees the openings rather than the obstacles, the good in any challenge, the light at the end of every tunnel, the sweet lemonade in every sour lemon.

Assignment. Search for options, and design and declare a breakthrough (either in your 100-Day Catalytic Project or elsewhere in your work/life) by using the 3-step process of the last three days (1. Declare the Breakdown, 2. Revisit your background commitment, 3. Search for options and declare a breakthrough). Debrief: what breakdown did you declare two days ago? What was your underlying commitment in the background yesterday? What is the breakthrough?

How did you do? To make declaring breakdowns second nature, some clients have made it a regular practice. For example, one leader declared a series of breakdowns to targeted colleagues each Friday before going into the weekend, to make sure that his colleagues would stay on their toes during the weekend. If you find that unfair, you could declare breakdowns each Monday to hit the week running.

Day 44: Action → Managing from Priorities

Date:_______

Without a deadline, baby,
I wouldn't do nothin'.
Duke Ellington

A key discipline that brings focus and serenity into your daily actions is, in one word: No. Someone who always says Yes is not a leader but a pinball of circumstances. Effective leaders have the discipline to say No. The Danish philosopher Søren Kierkegaard wrote: "Purity of the mind is to will one thing." What gives you real peace of mind is to focus on one thing: to prioritize and have the courage to say a well-reasoned No to lower-level priorities—even to demands that seem urgent or for which there is loud clamor. Take your cue from Jack Welch, who introduced just five major initiatives in his eighteen years as GE's chief executive; he simply refused to focus on other opportunities.

Clearly articulating and managing from priorities reduces what we call focus anxiety (constantly thinking of what you're *not* doing). No matter what a great leader you may be otherwise, working without priorities is like driving a car without a map or GPS and only a vague idea of where you want to go: You may drive as fast as you can and still not get there.

How you articulate your priorities determines their effectiveness as tools of accomplishment. Like promises and requests (as we saw on Day 37), unless priorities are clear and specific, you have a long shot at delivering them and might not even know whether you did. To be potent, a priority should begin with an action verb, be in time, and be measurable—or at least stated such that it will be clear whether you delivered it or not. The Table gives some examples.

Activities	Priorities
Improve sales performance.	Increase sales in each affiliate by 25+% this year.
Make more money.	Get board approval for a 5% raise by March 31.
Have more fun.	Go dancing at least twice this month.
Be a better father.	Read to the children for a half-hour a day.
Increase speed-to-market.	Double speed-to-market to under 120 days this year.

Assignment. Standing in your 5-year vision and your 100-day Catalytic Project, articulate potent, measurable priorities for this month and next week.

How did you do? If you're overwhelmed, chances are you are not focusing on your A1 priority. But be sure to articulate the priority such that it states what you really want. For example, "Call potential clients" is not an effective priority. If you call one prospect, have you done it? What if you called six prospects? Does it matter whether you actually reached them, or what you talked about when you called them? "Call potential clients" generates activity, not accomplishment. In contrast, "Generate at least requests for proposals this week" is clear and measurable. At the end of the week, there will be no question whether you have delivered the priority or not.

Day 45: Action → Displays

Date:_______

Everything should be made
as simple as possible,
but not simpler.
Albert Einstein

Productivity is a function not merely of commitment, but also of how you display your work. Displays are important for charting progress and building confidence, and vital to the success of any project. Usually we think of displays as visual reports, flipcharts, graphs, or posters on the wall. That's a good start, but there is much more. You could say that your entire environment is a set of displays that compel you to take certain actions, and that you can shape to support yourself in producing what you are committed to. Displays are indispensable tools for accomplishment. The right displays will compel you to take the highest-leverage actions, whether or not you are inspired or motivated.

If you are an illustrator who works at home, and your children constantly interrupt your work, they are part of your display that will pull for certain behaviors, such as trying to keep the kids quiet or avoiding phone calls for fear of them crying, which is bound to consume a large portion of your energy.

If you are a corporate executive and your office is always cluttered, that clutter is a display too, and it runs your work and life. What you look at every day determines the actions you take—even the actions you can think of taking. Because of the clutter, you take actions that you would not take were your office uncluttered. You probably focus on whatever is on top of the stack, no matter what the priority is—because you have little idea of what the priority is. There is no distinction between what is merely urgent and what is truly important. In the clutter, everything has equal priority until something becomes a crisis. Whatever is most urgent gets done. A display, on the other hand, helps you focus on what is important.

Executives at a bank discovered the power of two displays: They found that their call-center people's phone calls were more personable if they could drink coffee at their desks and if they looked into a mirror while talking to customers on the phone.

The best displays are creative, imaginative, and fun. In an end-of-the-year campaign, one organization put balloons up all around the office. People wore crazy hats, and each person had a whistle to blow whenever a sale was completed. A big chart on the wall showed a thermometer, with sales in green and revenue in blue. These displays were designed to replace seriousness and worry with unreasonable, playful action and the joy of results. It was a ball, and it worked: because of that campaign, the organization delivered a 17-percent increase in sales over the previous year.

Assignment. Take one key performance indicator given by your 5-year vision and/or your 100-Day Catalytic Project, and fashion a display that pulls for the right actions to achieve your goal along that indicator.

How did you do? A good display is whatever pulls for the highest-leverage actions. For a team leader, it could look something like this:

Team member	Target	Result so far	Likely result without intervention	Likely result with intervention	Intervention
John Doe	$1 million	$275k	$550,000	$850,000	Train in prospect qualification & active listening
Etc.					

What is the best place for your display, given your commitments and your situation? If you are a team leader, you may want to post the display on a flipchart or whiteboard right at the entrance of the office, or on your Intranet. If you are a highly mobile executive, you may want to keep your display inside your time planner, laptop, or smartphone. The point is to put the display where you will see it frequently. Your commitments need to be in your face. For example, my business partner Philippe has a commitment to drink water every hour, so he put an invisible calendar called "Water" in his calendar app as an hourly repeating event with an alarm attached to it. I have a similar daily reminder of three keywords that guide me ("Source of Power. Patient. Free"); the display shows up each day to remind me of who I am. It may sound a bit obsessive, but it works for building any new habit you want to build.

Day 46: Action → The Power of Details

Date:_______

In a race, a split second
can define the entire competition.
One tire length will decide
whether you are a winner or a loser.
If you understand that,
you cannot disregard
even the smallest improvement.
Soichiro Honda

If leadership is largely about accomplishment, what is at the heart of accomplishment? One word: detail. All great accomplishments are the sum of seemingly trivial details. There are no grand actions *per se*. When a head of state signs a history-making law, that action consists of nothing more than putting a pen to paper and signing a name. It is simply the culmination of countless trivial actions that preceded it.

Bill Gates is famous for putting his finger intuitively on unresolved details when executives present their ideas. This is how one Microsoft vice president explained his boss's ability to immerse himself in the details of his company:

> You may think you have everything totally prepared, and the one area you weren't quite sure about, somehow he just finds it right away, and asks you the one right question. He'll know intricate low-level detail about a program, and you wonder, "How does he know that? He has no reason ever to get to that level!" Some piece of code, or some other technology Microsoft isn't even involved in. You just shake your head.[18]

Other leaders feel that such "menial details" are beneath them, that trivialities should be delegated to others. That is exactly where things break down. Proven implementers like Jack Welch of General Electric or Larry Bossidy of Allied-Signal know this. Leaders like these do not end a meeting without first writing down exactly what will be done by whom and by when. They then go over the list of "who/what/when" before the meeting closes, and even send a reminder to each participant after the meeting. The very details that might bore others stimulate them to create and accomplish.

The Swiss have a proverb: *Wer den Rappen nicht ehrt, ist des Frankens nicht wert.* ("He who does not honor the cent is not worth the dollar.") For an accomplishment to measure up to the vision that inspired it, you have to attend to the details. Every detail should embody and reflect the strategic intent. CNN-founder Ted Turner knew that the details of communication needed to be aligned with his vision. On December 17, 1976, the same day he bought his first satellite uplink, he had his receptionist answer the phone by saying "The superstation that serves the nation." There is nothing that does not make a difference—the way you greet people when you walk down the hall, the way you complete a meeting, the mood you are in when you make a phone call. Everything is relevant. Anything can backfire.

It is in the details where the disagreements arise, where separation gains the upper hand. It is one thing to be aligned on a grand, inspiring vision; it is quite another to keep that alignment in the face of everyday operational challenges. Details have the power to destroy marriages and mergers, to cause warfare and wounds. Details count.

Assignment. Take the time today to attend to 3-5 details in your 100-Day Catalytic Project that you have neglected so far.

How did you do? Details may seem tedious but can pay off handsomely. A study conducted by Keilty, Goldsmith & Company involving more than 8,000 leaders in Fortune 100 companies found a direct correlation between follow-up and perceived leadership effectiveness. The message is clear: following through on the details makes all the difference between mediocre and great leaders.

Day 47: Action → Project Status

Date:_______

To undertake a project,
as the word's derivation indicates,
means to cast an idea out ahead of oneself
so that it gains autonomy and is fulfilled
not only by the efforts of its originator but,
indeed, independently of him as well.
Czeslaw Milosz

Managing your key performance indicators or priorities alone does not give you access to accomplishment. You have to learn managing the *energy* of your project. One simple way to do that is to assess where the project is:

Complete: The project succeeded (or failed), and it's over. What may be left to do is to debrief the project and communicate the success (or failure) to the respective people.

On Track: The project is on track to succeed without any intervention, i.e. if you continue business-as-usual.

Behind: The project will not succeed without intervention, but you know exactly what interventions to take to move the project back on track.

In Danger: The project will not succeed even with all the interventions you can take. You need a breakthrough process and major reallocation of organizational resources to move the project back on track and have it succeed.

Abandoned: The project is out of existence. You need a strategy meeting to revisit the original vision of the project, see why it went out of existence, see what's missing, and recommit to the project (or choose deliberately to discontinue it).

Assignment. Take your 100-Day Catalytic Project (or any project for that matter), and assess the status of the project. Then identify and take the steps to move the project to the next level.

How did you do? Many people assess their project status over-optimistically—until it's too late and they cannot salvage it anymore. You have to step back and take an honest and conservative look: The way it's going, is the project truly on track and will succeed with business-as-usual, or is it really behind or in danger, to tell the truth? Remember, it's not you who is behind or in danger; it's just the project. Calling a spade a spade does not reflect badly on you—quite the contrary.

Day 48: Action → Operating States

Date:_______

Everything is in transformation.
The rose that wilts after six days will become part of the garbage.
After six months the garbage is transformed into a rose.
When we speak of impermanence,
we understand that everything is in transformation.
This becomes that, and that becomes this.
Thich Nhat Hanh

In addition to assessing the status of a project, you can use a more sophisticated system of distinct stages through which any project (or even an entire company) can pass—a roadmap from start-up through sustainability. These *operating states*[19] put your hands on the levers and dials of the project; you know what actions are needed to take the project to the next level. We can distinguish five operating states:

Formulation is typically, but not always, the start of the project. It is the state of creation when you formulate the project, announce it, and declare your commitment to it. At this point you build a shared strategy for the project, clean things up, establish the lines of communication, determine what's needed, agree on the ground rules, and say what you can be counted on to produce.

Concentration is the eye of the needle through which any successful project must pass. This state is characterized by high input of energy, coupled with low output of results: you put ten units in but get only one out. Concentration gets its name from the attribute needed for success at this stage: concentrated attention and action, and virtually no discussion. This stage is characterized by intensity, toughness, and resilience. You need to grind out the results, eliminate unnecessary actions, and do what you said you would—no matter what the circumstances. This is the time to eliminate all alternatives to producing the results, box yourself in, and close the back door. Now you simply follow instructions and tighten the discipline. It is important to have a clear-cut statement of short-term results because you need some wins that sustain the morale of the team. Other factors essential for success include building trust among team members, promoting strengths, encouraging winning, and owning the project completely—especially when the going gets tough, as it usually does in this phase. Since Concentration can be grueling, make sure the drudgery does not last forever. Keep blocks of concentration finite, and interrupt them with breaks where the players can take care of their well-being—or simply get enough sleep before the next round.

Momentum, the operating state that comes next if and when you succeed with Concentration, is characterized by energy almost opposite that of Concentration. Now a low input of energy leads to a high output of results: one in, ten out. Spontaneity, inspiration, communication, and high activity are symptomatic of Momentum. After the intensity of Concentration, people's tendency will be to put their feet up. So it is essential to remain vigilant during Momentum. Nothing is won yet; you could just as easily slip back into the grueling state of concentration. Keep people focused on the overall accomplishment, not just on a specific result or on following instructions. Now is the time to mend any wounds left over from Concentration, complete loose ends, and monitor the discipline so that it does not vanish in the excitement. This is also the time to expand the project by promoting it and having people think well of it. In Momentum, it is essential to communicate the vision, to have a clear grasp on the numbers, and to manage the project to produce the numbers. Look for leverage by asking the question "What will make *the* difference?"

Breakthrough is the operating state in which things are working brilliantly. In addition to celebrating, this is the time to strengthen your ability to deliver and create a context for the final stage, Sustainability. Make sure a clear structure of communication and reporting is in place so you don't have to reinvent the wheel. Be vigilant—clean up any messes between people, "pay all bills" in a manner of speaking, put your house in order, and do anything else needed in the way of training and support.

Sustainability is the stage when the project has grown and is no longer like a baby that will die without constant vigilance and nurturing. Sustainability could have as its motto, "Don't mess with the luck." This is the time to institutionalize your structures and rules, and build a surplus for the future. To do that, you need to look at the whole and generate a vast, inspiring context. You also need to make the project self-generating by standardizing it; training, authorizing, and empowering more people; encouraging teamwork; devising statistics and displays; and providing definition, interfaces, procedures, and manuals as needed.

The point of these distinctions is to identify where you are so that you can provide what's missing to move to the next operating state. Having said that, note that the operating states are not sequential or linear, and not every project will necessarily move through all of them.

Physicists tell us that stability does not occur in nature and that chaos is the norm. Projects, like everything else in nature, are fluid. They progress and regress, ebb and flow. It is possible and even likely that a project slips at times, in which case you have to declare an emergency and throw resources at the project to move it up again.

Assignment. In which operating state is your 100-Day Catalytic Project at this moment? Again, be honest, even conservative, in your assessment, so you don't have to move back to an earlier operating state because of over-optimism. Now devise the intervention(s) that will move the project to the next operating state.

How did you do? You can learn to diagnose the current operating state by looking at the energy around you. For example, when you hear a lot of declarations and expressions of commitment from people, or when you get many questions about why the project exists at all or how it all works, you know that you are still in Formulation. If people put their nose the grindstone and it's hard work day after day, you know you are in Concentration. When results seem to come in unexpectedly and effortlessly, you know you are in Momentum.

Day 49: Action → Regular Practices

Date:_______

Don't try. Do.
Inscription at Harvard chemistry lab[20]

Routines don't have to be dull; they can be creative. Committed to improving the quality of its customer service, Citibank Privatkunden AG in Germany sought to cut waiting time for customers calling in from 20 seconds to 8 seconds. The bank instituted a practice for each employee to take five minutes on a given day to achieve a "wow" effect by exceeding one customer's expectations.

Bill Walsh, former head coach of the 49ers, said about regular drills:

> The most important tool for getting things done is the drill. For example, we work on drills to teach running backs about pass protection against blitz-running linebackers. You have to identify the 6 different situations that can occur. Then you have to allocate the time to work on those 6 situations and also the 20 techniques that you want your running backs to be able to apply…

Regular practices can be annual, quarterly, monthly, weekly, or daily. Here are some examples:

- **Annual:** On your birthday, take stock of your life accomplishment.
  At the end of each year, look at what worked and what didn't work during the previous year, acknowledge your accomplishments of the past year, and create your goals for the coming year.
  Every June, go for a medical check-up.
- **Monthly:** Review and update your displays of your progress toward major objectives.

Pay your bills on the first of each month.
Answer your overdue correspondence on Facebook and other networks on the 15th each month.

- **Weekly:** On Sundays, create your priorities for the coming week.
  On Mondays, declare what you will *not* do that week.
  On Wednesdays, finish unfinished business and take care of administrative details.
  On Thursdays, answer overdue correspondence.
  On Fridays, speculate about new possibilities.
  Schedule a cultural experience once a week.
- **Daily:** Meditate each morning.
  Take a walk each evening.
  Read something each day that gives you a new perspective.

Assignment. What practices, in any domain of your life, can you schedule regularly to prevent them from being dropped out of your life? What regular actions will fulfill your life? Determine exact dates and times for these practices, and put those dates and times in your time planning system.

- Annual:

- Quarterly:

- Monthly:

- Weekly:

- Daily:

How did you do? The trick is to have not only dull and tedious routine actions (like doing your taxes or flossing your teeth—although for some even these can be enjoyable and fulfilling), but routines that fulfill your life (like hiking or learning a new skillset or brainstorming whole new possibilities). For example, to spur innovation and original thinking, Google engineers are asked to spend one day each week working on something *outside of and unrelated to* Google.

Day 50: Action → Debriefs

Date:_______

Give me a lever long enough and a prop strong enough.
I can single-handedly move the world.
Archimedes

Debriefing a project is a skill and practice as important as the project itself, and essential for organizational learning. The word *debrief* derives from diplomacy, the military, and space aviation. *Webster's* defines it as "to interrogate (a soldier, astronaut, diplomat, etc.) on return from a mission in order to assess the conduct and results of the mission." Without debriefing, you run the risk of having to keep reinventing the wheel—that is, of not applying in the next project what you learned in the last one. It is important that you do not move on until the current project is complete, and a project is not complete until you have debriefed it.

In 1986, when I led a global campaign involving 27 countries worldwide, one of the smartest moves I made was to call the manager who had led the campaign the year before and ask him what had worked and not worked. I asked him what he would do again, what he would not repeat, and what he would now do that he had not done. Based on that relatively brief interview, I got so much information that I was able to stand on his experience, And I did not have to waste time figuring out how to do what had already been done.

Assignment. Take an important business meeting or project that ended recently, and debrief it. Answer:

- What was accomplished vis-à-vis your objectives? What else was accomplished? And what is the meaning of these accomplishments for your/your organization's mission?

- What was not accomplished?

- What worked? What were the key success factors?

- What did not work?

- What did you learn?

- What leaders emerged, and how could you empower them now?

- What opportunities emerged, and how could you capitalize on them?

- What unfinished business needs to be finished?

- Who needs to be acknowledged and for what, by whom, and how?

- Who should know about the accomplishment, and how will you let them know?

- What''s next?

- Anything else?

How did you do? Many leaders fall into the trap of finishing a project or event and either being so burned out that that they just want to forget about what happened, or being so eager to rush on to the next thing, that they can never fully capitalize on what happened. But debriefing a project or event is at least as important as doing it. Mahatma Gandhi walked to the Indian Ocean and picked up a handful of salt; but that action in and of itself would not have made the British Empire tremble. What made the action an historic building block of India's independence was how Gandhi brilliantly capitalized on the moment and made it a message that reverberated around the world.

Day 51: Action → Generating Distinctions

Date:_______

I can't understand why people
are frightened of new ideas.
I'm frightened of old ones.
John Cage

It is said that when the Renaissance artist Michelangelo created a sculpture, for example *David*, he saw the final statue already hidden in the rough un-hewn stone. All he had to do was to reveal the sculpture by taking away that which was *not* the sculpture. That is what we do whenever we create, and even when we lead a meeting: we distinguish what's on message or on purpose from what's *not*.

Leaders don't merely transfer information; they create distinctions that reframe what people see. What we see is a function of the distinctions we draw. Our actions are correlated not to what's in front of us, but to how we *see* what's in front of us. The actions we can see taking are a result of the distinctions we draw. Making distinctions is an intrinsic part of the process of creation. According to the Bible, in the first act of creation on earth, God drew a distinction:

> In the beginning God created the heavens and the earth—when the earth was astonishingly empty, with darkness upon the surface of the deep, and the Divine Presence hovered upon the surface of the waters—God said, "Let there be light," and there was light. God saw that the light was good, and God separated between the light and the darkness. God called to the light: "Day," and to the darkness he called: "Night," and there was evening and there was morning, one day.[21]

Those who have a rich body of distinctions in a given arena have power with respect to that arena. The more distinctions you draw, the more freedom of action you have, the more ability you have to create, and the more possibilities you have at your command. It is said that the Inuit can distinguish among 23 types of snow. For the Inuit, *snow* is of a rich body of distinctions, each of which calls for different actions. One kind of snow is for building igloos, another is good for fishing, another is treacherous. Inuit are effective in their hostile environment because of the distinctions they see.

Leaders who create and sustain extraordinary accomplishments constantly generate new distinctions among seemingly similar things. One Australian CEO can look at a company and see immediately what is wrong with its strategy—the way some auto mechanics can listen to an engine and know what is amiss. He can do that because of the distinctions he has access to. If you are confronting an issue, your power regarding that issue will increase as you draw distinctions about it.

Assignment. In your next meeting or phone call (on your 100-Day Catalytic Project or on another matter), see if you can draw distinctions within the conversation. (A simple set of distinctions is the Global Leader Pyramid®: are you or others in a conversation for Self-awareness, or Relationship, or Vision, or Strategy, or Action?)

How did you do? By now you will be able to draw clear distinctions among conversations you take part in: a conversation for Self-Awareness (for example, "Why is this important to me?"), Relationship ("Who are you?"), Vision ("What do you really want?"), Strategy ("How can we get there?") or Action ("When will you get it to me?"). The act of drawing distinctions gives you power. All you have done is distinguish among the seeming "Same As It Ever Was," to borrow the title of the Talking Heads song. "Same As It Ever Was" is the enemy of leadership.

Day 52: Action → Implementation

Date:_______

First you learn your instrument.
Then you forget all that shit and play.
Charlie Parker

Assignment. Revisit Day 4 and your work in that module. (You're welcome to revisit the preliminary Days 1-3 too, but no need.) Given your learnings from that day, what action can you take today to succeed in your 100-Day Catalytic Project?

Note: You are now beyond the half-way mark in your 100-Day Catalytic Project. Today through Day 96 will focus on revisiting and deepening your work of the earlier days and implementing your Catalytic Project. Days 97-100 will focus on sustaining and institutionalizing your momentum. Use this second half of the 100-Day process to consolidate your learnings from the first half. For example, on Day 52, today, you revisit and consolidate your learnings from Day 4; on Day 53 from Day 5; and so forth. Revisiting your earlier learnings will enable you to integrate them fully in your day-to-day management and leadership game.

Day 53: Action → Implementation

Date:_______

We make a living by what we get,
but we make a life by what we give.
Winston Churchill

Assignment. Revisit Day 5 and your work in that module. Given your learnings from that day, what action can you take today to succeed in your 100-Day Catalytic Project?

Day 54: Action → Implementation

Date:_______

I never looked behind me to find out
what other people were playing or doing.
I just keep going, looking for new ideas, practicing...
I am never bored. There is always a new way to play anything.
Dizzy Gillespie

Assignment. Revisit Day 6 and your work in that module. Given your learnings from that day, what action can you take today to succeed in your 100-Day Catalytic Project?

Day 55: Action → Implementation

Date:_______

The rush and pressure of modern life are a form,
perhaps the most common form, of its innate violence.
To allow oneself to be carried away
by a multitude of conflicting concerns,
to surrender to too many demands,
to commit oneself to too many projects,
to want to help everyone in everything
is to succumb to violence.
More than that, it is cooperation in violence.
The frenzy of the activist neutralizes his or her work,
because it kills the root and inner wisdom
which makes work fruitful.
Thomas Merton

Assignment. Revisit Day 7 and your work in that module. Given your learnings from that day, what action can you take today to succeed in your 100-Day Catalytic Project?

Day 56: Action → Implementation

Date:_______

The feeling of being hurried is not usually the result
of living a full life and having no time.
It is, to the contrary, born of the vague fear
that we are wasting our life.
When we do not do the thing that we ought to do,
we have no time for anything else.
Eric Hoffer

Assignment. Revisit Day 8 and your work in that module. Given your learnings from that day, what action can you take today to succeed in your 100-Day Catalytic Project?

Day 57: Action → Implementation

Date:_______

All means prove but a blunt instrument
if they have not behind them a living spirit.
But if the longing for achievement of the goal
is powerfully alive within us,
then we shall not lack the strength
to find the means for reaching the goal
and for translating it into deeds.
Albert Einstein

Assignment. Revisit Day 9 and your work in that module. Given your learnings from that day, what action can you take today to succeed in your 100-Day Catalytic Project?

Day 58: Action → Implementation

Date:_______

Purity of the mind is to will one thing.
Søren Kierkegaard

Assignment. Revisit Day 10 and your work in that module. Given your learnings from that day, what action can you take today to succeed in your 100-Day Catalytic Project?

Day 59: Action → Implementation

Date:_______

Almost anybody can learn to think or believe or know,
but not a single human being can be taught to be. Why?
Because whenever you think or you believe you know,
you are a lot of other people;
but the moment you are being, you're nobody-but-yourself.
To be nobody-but-yourself –
in a world which is doing its best night and day
to make you everybody else –
means to fight the hardest battle
which any human being can fight,
and never stop fighting.
Does this sound dismal? It isn't.
It's the most wonderful life on earth.
e.e. cummings

Assignment. Revisit Day 11 and your work in that module. Given your learnings from that day, what action can you take today to succeed in your 100-Day Catalytic Project?

Day 60: Action → Implementation

Date:_______

A conclusion is the place
where you got tired thinking.
Martin H. Fischer

Assignment. Revisit Day 12 and your work in that module. Given your learnings from that day, what action can you take today to succeed in your 100-Day Catalytic Project?

Day 61: Action → Implementation

Date:_______

True belonging is born of relationships
not only to one another
but to a place of shared responsibilities and benefits.
We love not so much what we have acquired
as what we have made
and with whom we have made it.
Robert Finch

Assignment. Revisit Day 13 and your work in that module. Given your learnings from that day, what action can you take today to succeed in your 100-Day Catalytic Project?

Day 62: Action → Implementation

Date:_______

When spider webs unite,
they can tie up a lion.
Ethiopian Proverb

Assignment. Revisit Day 14 and your work in that module. Given your learnings from that day, what action can you take today to succeed in your 100-Day Catalytic Project?

Day 63: Action → Implementation

Date:_______

Let no one say that he is a follower of Gandhi.
It is enough that I should be my own follower.
You are not followers but fellow students,
fellow pilgrims, fellow seekers, fellow workers.
Mahatma Gandhi

Assignment. Revisit Day 15 and your work in that module. Given your learnings from that day, what action can you take today to succeed in your 100-Day Catalytic Project?

Day 64: Action → Implementation

Date:_______

Theorists conduct experiments with their brains.
Experimenters have to use their hands, too.
Theorists are thinkers, experimenters are craftsmen.
The theorist needs no accomplice.
The experimenter has to muster graduate students,
cajole machinists, flatter lab assistants.
The theorist operates in a pristine place
free of noise, of vibration, of dirt.
The experimenter develops an intimacy with matter
as a sculptor does with clay, battling it,
shaping it and engaging it.
The theorist invents his companions,
as a naïve Romeo imagined his ideal Juliet.
The experimenter's lovers sweat, complain, and fart.
James Gleick

Assignment. Revisit Day 16 and your work in that module. Given your learnings from that day, what action can you take today to succeed in your 100-Day Catalytic Project?

Day 65: Action → Implementation

Date:_______

There is a vitality, a life force, a quickening
that is translated through you into action,
and because there is only one of you in all time,
this expression is unique.
If you block it, it will never exist
through any other medium and be lost.
The world will not have it.
It is not your business to determine how good it is;
nor how valuable it is;
nor how it compares with other expressions.
It is your business to keep it yours,
clearly and directly, to keep the channel open.
You do not even have to believe in yourself or your work.
You have to keep open and aware directly
to the urges that motivate you.
Keep the channel open. No artist is pleased.
There is no satisfaction whatever at any time.
There is only a queer, divine dissatisfaction;
a blessed unrest that keeps us marching
and makes us more alive than the others.
Martha Graham

Assignment. Revisit Day 17 and your work in that module. Given your learnings from that day, what action can you take today to succeed in your 100-Day Catalytic Project?

Day 66: Action → Implementation

Date:_______

The meeting of two personalities
is like the contact of two chemical substances;
if there is any reaction, both are transformed.
Carl Gustav Jung

Assignment. Revisit Day 18 and your work in that module. Given your learnings from that day, what action can you take today to succeed in your 100-Day Catalytic Project?

Day 67: Action → Implementation

Date:_______

To love things as they are would be a mockery of things:
a true lover must love them as they would wish to be.
For nothing is quite happy as it is,
and the first act of true sympathy must be
to move with the object of love towards its happiness.
George Santayana

Assignment. Revisit Day 19 and your work in that module. Given your learnings from that day, what action can you take today to succeed in your 100-Day Catalytic Project?

Day 68: Action → Implementation

Date:_______

This is the true joy in life,
the being used for a purpose
recognized by yourself as a mighty one,
the being a force of nature instead of a feverish,
selfish little clod of ailments and grievances
complaining that the world
will not devote itself to making you happy.
I am of the opinion that my life belongs
to the whole community
and as long as I live
it is my privilege to do for it whatever I can.
I want to be thoroughly used up when I die,
for the harder I work the more I live.
I rejoice in life for its own sake.
Life is no "brief candle" to me.
It is a sort of splendid torch
which I have got a hold of for the moment,
and I want to make it burn as brightly as possible
before handing it on to future generations.
George Bernard Shaw

Assignment. Revisit Day 20 and your work in that module. Given your learnings from that day, what action can you take today to succeed in your 100-Day Catalytic Project?

Day 69: Action → Implementation

Date:_______

I was born not knowing
and have only had a little time
to change that here and there.
Richard Feynman

Assignment. Revisit Day 21 and your work in that module. Given your learnings from that day, what action can you take today to succeed in your 100-Day Catalytic Project?

Day 70: Action → Implementation

Date:_______

If we quarrel with the past,
we may lose the future.
Winston Churchill

Assignment. Revisit Day 22 and your work in that module. Given your learnings from that day, what action can you take today to succeed in your 100-Day Catalytic Project?

Day 71: Action → Implementation

Date:_______

There are at least two kinds of games.
One could be called finite, the other infinite.
A finite game is played for the purpose of winning,
an infinite game for the purpose of continuing the play.
The rules of the finite game may not change;
the rules of an infinite game must change.
Finite players play within boundaries;
infinite players play with boundaries.
Finite players are serious;
infinite games are playful.
A finite player plays to be powerful;
an infinite player plays with strength.
Finite games can be played within an infinite game,
but an infinite game cannot be played within a finite game.
A finite player consumes time;
an infinite player generates time.
The finite player aims for eternal life;
the infinite player aims for eternal birth.
James Carse

Assignment. Revisit Day 23 and your work in that module. Given your learnings from that day, what action can you take today to succeed in your 100-Day Catalytic Project?

Day 72: Action → Implementation

Date:_______

Destiny is not a matter of chance,
it is a matter of choice.
William Jennings Bryan

Assignment. Revisit Day 24 and your work in that module. Given your learnings from that day, what action can you take today to succeed in your 100-Day Catalytic Project?

Day 73: Action → Implementation

Date:_______

Only in two humans of whom each,
when he means the other,
means simultaneously
the highest meaning for the other,
and serves the fulfillment of that meaning,
without wanting to impose on the other
something of his own realization,
the dynamic glory of the human essence
presents itself bodily.
Martin Buber

Assignment. Revisit Day 25 and your work in that module. Given your learnings from that day, what action can you take today to succeed in your 100-Day Catalytic Project?

Day 74: Action → Implementation

Date:_______

Without belittling the courage with which men have died,
we should not forget those acts of courage
with which men have lived.
The courage of life is often a less dramatic spectacle
than the courage of a final moment;
but it is no less a magnificent mixture of triumph and tragedy.
A man does what he must – in spite of personal consequences,
in spite of obstacles, dangers, and pressure –
and that is the basis of all human morality.
John F. Kennedy

Assignment. Revisit Day 26 and your work in that module. Given your learnings from that day, what action can you take today to succeed in your 100-Day Catalytic Project?

Day 75: Action → Implementation

Date:_______

My life is an indivisible whole,
and all my activities run into one another;
and they all have their rise
in my insatiable love of mankind.
Mahatma Gandhi

Assignment. Revisit Day 27 and your work in that module. Given your learnings from that day, what action can you take today to succeed in your 100-Day Catalytic Project?

Day 76: Action → Implementation

Date:_______

A hundred times everyday I remind myself
that my inner and outer life
depend on the labors of other men,
living and dead,
and that I must exert myself
in order to give
in the measure as I have received
and am still receiving.
Albert Einstein

Assignment. Revisit Day 28 and your work in that module. Given your learnings from that day, what action can you take today to succeed in your 100-Day Catalytic Project?

Day 77: Action → Implementation

Date:_______

Most of the things worth doing in the world
had been declared impossible before they were done.
Louis D. Brandeis

Assignment. Revisit Day 29 and your work in that module. Given your learnings from that day, what action can you take today to succeed in your 100-Day Catalytic Project?

Day 78: Action → Implementation

Date:_______

We have to renounce a description of phenomena based on the concept of cause and effect.
Niels Bohr

Assignment. Revisit Day 30 and your work in that module. Given your learnings from that day, what action can you take today to succeed in your 100-Day Catalytic Project?

Day 79: Action → Implementation

Date:_______

Give all thou canst;
high Heaven rejects the nicely calculated
less or more.
William Wordsworth

Assignment. Revisit Day 31 and your work in that module. Given your learnings from that day, what action can you take today to succeed in your 100-Day Catalytic Project?

Day 80: Action → Implementation

Date:_______

He must sacrifice his little will,
which is unfree and ruled by things and drives,
to his great will that moves away
from being determined to find destiny.
Now he no longer interferes,
nor does he merely allow things to happen.
He listens to that which grows,
to the way of Being in the world,
not in order to be carried along by it
but rather in order to actualize it
in the manner in which it, needing him,
wants to be actualized by him –
with human spirit and human deed,
with human life and human death.
He believes, I said: but this implies:
he encounters.
Martin Buber

Assignment. Revisit Day 32 and your work in that module. Given your learnings from that day, what action can you take today to succeed in your 100-Day Catalytic Project?

Day 81: Action → Implementation

Date:_______

I want to know what you will do about it.
I do not want to know what you hope.
I want to know what you will work for.
I do not want your sympathy for the needs of humanity.
I want your muscle.
As the wagon driver said when they came to a long, hard hill,
"Them that's going on with us, get out and push.
Them that ain't, get out of the way."
Robert Fulghum

Assignment. Revisit Day 33 and your work in that module. Given your learnings from that day, what action can you take today to succeed in your 100-Day Catalytic Project?

Day 82: Action → Implementation

Date:_______

Mistakes are almost always of a sacred nature.
Never try to correct them.
Salvador Dali

Assignment. Revisit Day 34 and your work in that module. Given your learnings from that day, what action can you take today to succeed in your 100-Day Catalytic Project?

Day 83: Action → Implementation

Date:_______

The only thing standing
between greatness and me,
is me.
Woody Allen

Assignment. Revisit Day 35 and your work in that module. Given your learnings from that day, what action can you take today to succeed in your 100-Day Catalytic Project?

Day 84: Action → Implementation

Date:_______

The people who give the most are the most alive.
They laugh – literally laugh –
at the notion that they are somehow diminished
for the "sacrifice" of their service.
Gary Gunderson

Assignment. Revisit Day 36 and your work in that module. Given your learnings from that day, what action can you take today to succeed in your 100-Day Catalytic Project?

Day 85: Action → Implementation

Date:_______

The difficult we will do right away.
The impossible may take a little longer.
Billie Holiday

Assignment. Revisit Day 37 and your work in that module. Given your learnings from that day, what action can you take today to succeed in your 100-Day Catalytic Project?

Day 86: Action → Implementation

Date:_______

What is a good man but a bad man's teacher?
What is a bad man but a good man's job?
If you don't understand this, you will get lost,
however intelligent you are.
It is the great secret.
Lao Tzu

Assignment. Revisit Day 38 and your work in that module. Given your learnings from that day, what action can you take today to succeed in your 100-Day Catalytic Project?

Day 87: Action → Implementation

Date:_______

Do not be the possessor of fame.
Do not be the storehouse of schemes.
Do not take over the function of things.
Do not be the master of knowledge.
Personally realize the infinite to the highest degree
and travel in the realm of which there is no sign.
Exercise fully what you have received from Nature
without any subjective viewpoint.
In one word, be absolutely vacuous.
Chuang Tzu

Assignment. Revisit Day 39 and your work in that module. Given your learnings from that day, what action can you take today to succeed in your 100-Day Catalytic Project?

Day 88: Action → Implementation

Date:_______

After the final no, there comes a yes
and on that yes the future of the world depends.
Wallace Stevens

Assignment. Revisit Day 40 and your work in that module. Given your learnings from that day, what action can you take today to succeed in your 100-Day Catalytic Project?

Day 89: Action → Implementation

Date:_______

People are always blaming their circumstances
for what they are.
I don't believe in circumstances.
The people who get on in this world
are the people who get up
and look for the circumstances they want,
and, if they can't find them, make them.
George Bernard Shaw

Assignment. Revisit Day 41 and your work in that module. Given your learnings from that day, what action can you take today to succeed in your 100-Day Catalytic Project?

Day 90: Action → Implementation

Date:_______

Not happiness makes us grateful,
but gratitude makes us happy.
David Steindl-Rast

Assignment. Revisit Day 42 and your work in that module. Given your learnings from that day, what action can you take today to succeed in your 100-Day Catalytic Project?

Day 91: Action → Implementation

Date:_______

There are many who can execute
and display magnificent fireworks;
but who knows how to kindle
a spark in the darkness of the soul?
Abraham J. Heschel

Assignment. Revisit Day 43 and your work in that module. Given your learnings from that day, what action can you take today to succeed in your 100-Day Catalytic Project?

Day 92: Action → Implementation

Date:_______

If I don't manage to fly, someone else will.
The spirit wants only that there be flying.
As for who happens to do it,
In that he has only a passing interest.
Rainer Maria Rilke

Assignment. Revisit Day 44 and your work in that module. Given your learnings from that day, what action can you take today to succeed in your 100-Day Catalytic Project?

Day 93: Action → Implementation

Date:_______

When you are a winner,
you have to set the standard for excellence wherever you go.
You have to battle against the fatigue, the intimidation,
the human tendency to just want to take things a little easier.
You have to be able to come up with, time and time again,
one consistently great performance after another.
It's grueling. And I don't know how many people
are willing to make the effort.
But it's those few true professionals
you meet along the way that help
make the journey just a little easier to manage.
Martina Navratilova

Assignment. Revisit Day 45 and your work in that module. Given your learnings from that day, what action can you take today to succeed in your 100-Day Catalytic Project?

Day 94: Action → Implementation

Date:_______

The world revolts against the order imposed on it by the brain.
The more it is forced, with rigor and impatience,
into rational categories,
the greater are the explosions of irrationality
with which it surprises us…
One cannot fool a plant any more
than one can fool history.
But one can water it.
Patiently, every day.
With understanding, with humility,
but also with love.
Vaclav Havel

Assignment. Revisit Day 46 and your work in that module. Given your learnings from that day, what action can you take today to succeed in your 100-Day Catalytic Project?

Day 95: Action → Implementation

Date:______

Never give in, never, never, never
in nothing, great or small – never give in
except to convictions of honor and good sense.
Winston Churchill

Assignment. Revisit Day 47 and your work in that module. Given your learnings from that day, what action can you take today to succeed in your 100-Day Catalytic Project?

Day 96: Action → Implementation

Date:_______

When I have finished,
if the solution is not beautiful,
I know it is wrong.
Buckminster Fuller

Assignment. Revisit Day 48-51 and your work in those modules. Given your learnings from those days, what actions can you take today to succeed in your 100-Day Catalytic Project?

Day 97: Sustainability → Basics

Date:_______

Whenever an individual or a business decides that success has been attained, progress stops.
Thomas Watson

You are now coming to the final stretch of your 100-Day Catalytic Project. Now it's time to focus on sustaining your momentum. The question of sustainability is one of the toughest questions leaders must confront. One mistake that leaders often make is to assume that once they produce an accomplishment, things will stay that way. They won't. Things change. Asked what he has learned from Jack Welch, his successor at General Electric Jeff Immelt replied that business presents no easy answers, only a succession of sub-optimal solutions that must be worked at, then rethought and worked at again.[22]

Whether he was aware of it or not, Immelt was talking about entropy. Entropy is the natural tendency of things to lose their distinctness and become indistinguishable. Entropy is the opposite of creating distinctions. The result is a soup of undistinguished stuff. What was a perfect intervention yesterday has blended into the wallpaper today and is indistinguishable from current practice.

We have all seen the results of entropy. Have you noticed how people look more and more like their dogs as years go by? (Just kidding.) Entropy occurs when you leave a garden alone for a while: eventually, everything in it will become like everything else. Desks are another case in point: your desktop never stays the same. You clean it up; it gets messy. No matter how often you put it in order, it will go back to chaos. Entropy happens in organizational settings, too: the policies and strategies that seem crystal clear at the top become muddled as they filter down into the organization. Business relationships become murky over time if they are not continuously deepened and re-created. Staff agreements are not kept. Requests are forgotten.

Assignment. Identify one feature of your 100-Day Catalytic Project that will fall prey to entropy unless you sustain it. Now institutionalize that feature, e.g. by putting a routine action into your calendar or time planning system.

How did you do? Life is a constant process of creation and destruction. Everything ebbs and flows. Nothing ever stays the same. Stability is an illusion. All things, from the moon to your muscles to the economy, expand or contract, wax or wane. Every day, your teeth need to be cleaned, your bed made, and the dishes washed. Every month, there are bills to pay, mail to answer, people to meet. If leaders expect something different, their expectations are inappropriate. Sustainability may elude them as leaders unless they take entropy into account.

Day 98: Sustainability → Eliminating Clutter

Date:_______

Order is intelligence.
Johann Wolfgang von Goethe

One form of entropy is clutter. *Webster's* defines clutter as "a jumble; confusion; disorder." The word comes from the Middle English *clot* and the Anglo-Saxon *clott,* meaning a "round mass." Like a clot, clutter consists of amassed things that were once distinct.

Eliminating clutter from your environment is crucial to leadership, accomplishment, and sustainability. Clutter builds up automatically, on a daily basis. Clutter muddles your mind, whether you're aware of it or not. If you live amid clutter for a long time, it recedes into the background, and you lose awareness of what is around you. But the clutter piles up nonetheless, taking up room and obscuring your vision. Often we waste more energy averting our eyes from clutter than it would take to eliminate the clutter.

What to do? The answer is simple but not easy: Surround yourself with only those things that you need to do a particular job. When you have completed the job, put the things relevant to the job away; then take out only what you need for the next job. And so on.

All things left alone tend to become clutter, even if they are not disordered or confused. Over time, documents and files turn stale and assume unnecessary weight and volume. This is a natural tendency, which you can counteract by reviewing all your information periodically. Identify what in your environment has become clutter. This means going through everything—hanging files, computer files, stacks of paper, and books. See whether the distinctions in which you have ordered your paperwork are still useful for the accomplishment you want to achieve.

Books can become clutter even when they are lined up neatly on a shelf. Over time, you do not even notice them anymore. I have fascinating leadership biographies that suddenly jumped out at me while I was writing this WorkBook. I had not noticed them for years. They were not disorderly. Always in full view, they were nonetheless hidden to my eyes. They had receded into the background.

Assignment. Go through one area at your office, for example a file cabinet or several notebooks, and bring them current. Keep only what you need now or for the future. Toss anything that is obsolete or no longer relevant. Decide what to do with things that are not obsolete. Put old information into archives or storage; keep in active files only that which feeds energy to your current activities and projects. Things will suddenly jump to life again, like glorious phoenixes arising from the dust.

How did you do? If you keep your financial paperwork in hanging files, are those files current or are there still invoices and receipts from years ago? The point of eliminating clutter is to stay on top of your information, to breathe life into it regularly. Eliminating clutter will forward your purpose and unearth ideas for the future. Everything in your work environment should be filled with life and purpose. Keep nothing around you that is devoid of future.

Day 99: Sustainability → Fire Yourself

Date:_______

I hate quotations.
Just tell me what you know.
Ralph Waldo Emerson

One of the responsibilities of leaders is succession strategy: to make sure the organization works and achieves its mission after their departure. But many leaders' ego gets in the way: They feel the world will collapse unless they stick around to save the day. They feel they are indispensible. They need to be needed. They might get addicted to the perks or the power. But unless you hand over your existing job, you will keep people down; and you will have a hard time moving on to what's next for you.

A healthy practice (and one likely to free you up) is to imagine—after you have created your strategy, action plan, or campaign—that you will not be around to see the project through to its end or to save the day if things go wrong. Identify what would be missing without you. For example, who would call people on their blind-spots or take responsibility for things that don't work? Who would cultivate key relationships? Who would sustain the vision and inspire people? Who would reshape the strategy? Who would mobilize people for action or display the results?

Assignment. Fill in the grid below. Identify your accountabilities (e.g. for strategy, for product development, etc.); your skills (e.g. facilitating global teleconferences, writing proposals, etc.); energies you uniquely provide (e.g. a can-do spirit, questioning assumptions or group-think, humor, etc.); and key relationships you hold (e.g. to key clients, to regulatory/government officials, to strategic vendors etc.). Once you have written down all items in these four domains, identify the person or people who could take charge of each item. Finally, identify your next action step to turn over each item and be sure to put a deadline for that action.

Domain	Items to Hand Over	To Whom?	Next Step/By When
Accountabilities			
Skills			
Energies			
Relationships			

How did you do? When clients of mine systematically list their accountabilities, skills, energies, and relationships, it reveals their total contribution to the company. The process of identifying these items and turning them over to specific colleagues is usually liberating. The leader is freed up to move on to their next challenge.

Day 100: Sustainability → 100-Day Debrief

Date:_______

As for the best leaders,
the people do not notice their existence.
The next best leaders, the people admire.
The next, the people fear,
and the next the people hate.
But when the best leader's work is done,
the people say, "We did it ourselves."
Lao Tzu (500 BCE)

Congratulations! You have now reached the 100th day, the completion of this WorkBook. But remember, this is only a tiny fraction of your journey as a leader. Leadership is not something that you can cross off on your checklist; it is not a task. Rather, it is an exploration of what it truly means to be a leader—as a life-long exploration.

The WorkBook followed the framework of the Global Leader Pyramid® (Self-Knowledge, Relationship, Vision, Strategy, Action); but the Pyramid is not merely a didactic tool. If you apply the Pyramid to your life and work, every day, week and year, and especially if you continue to make use of the breakdown-to-breakthrough methodology of Days 37-39, you will be virtually unstoppable. The mantra to keep in mind is this: nothing, and no-one, can disrupt your intention.

Assignment. Debrief your 100-Day Catalytic Project by answering the questions below. (Remember to do this regularly in the future, e.g. whenever you reach a key milestone or on the 1st of each month.)

What 3-5 year vision this project was designed to catalyze:

What were my project goals (measurable / specific / challenging / achievable / understandable / consistent with my goals, mission, principles) in the last 60-100 days:

What I accomplished:

What I did not accomplish:

What worked:

What did not work:

What opportunities showed up:

What leaders showed up:

Given my answers above, what is next:

How did you do? Very well, no doubt! I hope you can take pride in your accomplishments and results, while at the same time seeing areas for future work that demands your leadership. It has been a pleasure to work with you these past 100 days, and you have my very best wishes for continued success. May your leadership soar, may you be both ethical and effective as a leader, and may you make the difference that is uniquely yours to make.

A Call to Action: What Are You Gonna Do About It?

The great end of life is not knowledge but action.
—Huxley, Thomas H.

OK, now you have (presumably) read and worked through *Leadership in 100 Days*. The book has given you new insights. But those insights will evaporate as quickly as when you breathe out in the cold winter air—like a puff of steam. The only thing that will matter is ***action***. So here is a little debrief exercise designed to apply and sustain the learning.

What are the three most important learnings from this book that you can use in your life as a leader and/or manager? Practically speaking, What are three things you plan to start doing / stop doing / do differently based on reading this book?

1.
2.
3.

Please post your answer as a book review on the Amazon book page: https://amzn.to/2RCKfC1

If for any reason you feel uncomfortable making your answer public, post a brief review anyway—just one or two sentences about what difference the book made to you and your leadership. I'd love to see your feedback. Thank you!

And since all of this is but a conversation (but we know that conversations become reality), to continue the dialogue, connect to me on LinkedIn: https://www.linkedin.com/in/thomasdzweifel/

I am especially interested in seeing your best practices in applying the book to your life and work. And yes, your worst practices too, since we can all learn from failures, as we saw above. Meanwhile, here's to your success.

Further Readings & Resources

If you are not part of the solution,
then you are part of the problem.
Eldridge Cleaver

On Self-Awareness:

Argyris, Chris. 1991. "Teaching Smart People How to Learn," *Harvard Business Review*, May-June. 99-109.

Berne, Eric. [1964] 2004. *Games People Play: The Basic Handbook of Transactional Analysis.* New York: Random House.

Collins, Jim. 2001. *Good to Great.* New York: HarperBusiness.

Covey, Stephen R. 1991. *Principle-Centered Leadership.* New York: Summit Books.

Drucker, Peter F. 1999. "Managing Oneself," *Harvard Business Review*, March-April. 65-74.

Erhard, Werner, Michael C Jensen and Steve Zaffron. 2007. "Integrity: a Positive Model that Incorporates the Normative Phenomena of Morality, Ethics and Legality." Harvard NOM Working Paper No. 06-11. http://ssrn.com/abstract=920625

Goleman, Daniel. 1995. *Emotional Intelligence.* New York: Bantam Books.

_______. 2004. "What Makes a Leader?" *Harvard Business Review*, January 2004. 82-91.

Heidegger, Martin. 1968. *What Is Called Thinking?* Transl. by J. Glenn Gray. New York: Harper & Row.

Hofstede, Geert. 2001. *Culture's Consequences: Comparing Values, Behaviors, Institutions and Organizations Across Nations.* (2nd ed.) Thousand Oaks, CA: Sage Publications.

Kahneman, Daniel, Andrew M. Rosenfield, Linnea Gandhi and Tom Blaser. 2016. "Noise: How to Overcome to High, Hidden Costs of Inconsistent Decision-Making," *Harvard Business Review*, October.

Lukes, Steven. 1974. *Power: A Radical View*. London: Macmillan.

Messick, David M. and Max H. Bazerman, "Ethical Leadership and the Psychology of Decision Making," *Sloan Management Review*, Winter 1996, 9-22.

Snowden, David J. and Mary E. Boone. 2007. "A Leader's Framework for Decision-Making," *Harvard Business Review*, November.

Zweifel, Thomas D. 2013. *Culture Clash 2: Managing the Global High-Performance Team. New York*: SelectBooks.

On Relationship:

Buber, Martin. [1957] 1970. *I and Thou*. New York: Charles Scribner's Sons.

Flores, Fernando, and Terry Winograd. 1986. Understanding Computers and Cognition. Norwood NJ: Ablex Publishing Corporation.

Groysberg, Boris and Michael Slind. 2012. "Leadership Is a Conversation," *Harvard Business Review*. June.

Handy, Charles. 1995. "Trust and the Virtual Organization," *Harvard Business Review*, May-June. 40-50.

Katzenbach, J.R. and Smith, D.K. 1993. *The Wisdom of Teams: Creating the High-Performance Organization*. Cambridge MA: Harvard Business School.Press.

Magids, Scott, Alan Zorfas and Daniel Leemon. 2015. "The New Science of Customer Emotions," *Harvard Business Review*, November.

Perlow, Leslie A. 2003. *When You Say Yes But Mean No: How Silencing Conflict Wrecks Relationships and Companies… and What You Can Do About It*. New York: Crown Business.

Schulz von Thun, Friedemar. 1981. *Miteinander Reden: Störungen und Klärungen: Psychologie der zwischenmenschlichen Kommunikation*. Hamburg: Rowohlt.

Solomon, Robert C. and Fernando Flores. 2001. *Building Trust: In Business, Politics, Relationships, and Life*. Oxford: Oxford University Press.

Zweifel, Thomas D. 2003. *Communicate or Die: Getting Results Through Speaking and Listening.* New York: SelectBooks.

On Vision:

Bennis, Warren G. and Burt Nanus. 1985. *Leaders: The Strategies for Taking Charge*. New York: Harper & Row.

Carse, James P. 1987. *Finite and Infinite Games.* New York: Ballantine.

Goldberg, Florian und Michael Haensch. 2004. *Auf Welche Gipfel Wollen Sie?* Berlin: Lardon Media AG.

Goss, Tracy, Richard Pascale, and Anthony Athos. 1993. "The Reinvention Roller Coaster: Risking the Present for a Powerful Future," *HBR* Reprint #93603.

On Strategy:

Ancona, Deborah, Thomas Kochan, Maureen Scully, John Van Maanen, D. Eleanor Westney. 1996. *Managing for the Future*, Module 11: "Managing Change in Organizations." 1-54. Cincinnati OH: South-Western College Publishing.

Beer, Michael, Russell A. Eisenstat and Bert Spector. 1990. "Why Change Programs Don't Produce Change." *HBR* Reprint # 90601, 158-166.

Doz, Yves, José Santos and Peter Williamson. 2001. *From Global to Metanational: How Companies Win the Knowledge Economy*. Cambridge: Harvard Business School Press.

Hamel, Gary. 1996. "Strategy as Revolution," *Harvard Business Review*, July-August. 69-82.

Hamel, Gary and C.K. Prahalad. 1989. "Strategic Intent," *HBR* Reprint #89308 (May-Jun), 63-76.

Machiavelli, Niccoló. 1961. *The Prince*. London: Penguin Classics.

Prahalad, C.K. 2004. *The Fortune at the Bottom of the Pyramid.* Philadelphia: Wharton School Publishing.

Prahalad, C.K. and Kenneth Lieberthal. 1997. "The End of Corporate Imperialism," *Harvard Business Review* reprint 98408.

Sun Tzu. [500 BCE] 1963. *The Art of War.* Translated and with an introduction by Samuel B. Griffith. London: Oxford University Press.

The Hunger Project. 1991. "Planning-in-Action: an innovative approach to human development." New York: The Hunger Project. http://www.thp.org/programs/index.html

Zweifel, Thomas D. and Edward J. Borey. 2014. *Strategy-In-Action: Marrying Planning, People and Performance.* New York: iHorizon.

On Action/Sustainability:

Flaherty, James. 1999. *Coaching: Evoking Excellence in Others.* Boston: Butterworth-Heinemann.

Scherr, Allan L. 2005. "Managing for Breakthroughs in Productivity," Barbados Group Working Paper No. 1-05. Available at http://ssrn.com/abstract=655822

Sull, Donald N. and Charles Spinosa. 2007. "Promise-Based Management," Harvard Business Review, April.

Zweifel, Thomas D. and Aaron L. Raskin. 2008. *The Rabbi and the CEO: The Ten Commandments for 21st Century Leaders.* New York: SelectBooks.

The Author

Dr. Thomas D. Zweifel is a strategy & performance expert, board member & sparring partner for CEOs & leaders of Fortune 500 companies. The ex-CEO of Swiss Consulting Group, named "Fast Company" by *Fast Company* magazine, has coached clients on 4 continents since 1984 to open strategic frontiers, meet business imperatives and seize growth opportunities. An authority on integrating planning, people and performance, Thomas helps clients ask the right questions, confront taboos, build strategy alignment, and boost productivity. Ultimately his specialty is unleashing the human spirit in organizations—without unnecessary blah-blah, impractical training programs, or false dependencies on high-priced consultants.

Selected corporate clients: Airbus, Banana Republic, Citibank, ConocoPhillips, Credit Suisse, Danone, Dell, Deutsche Bank, DHL, Faurecia, Fiat, GE, GM, Goldman Sachs, Google, J&J, JPMorgan Chase, Medtronic, Nestlé, Novartis, P&G, Prudential, Roche, Sanofi, Siemens, Starbucks, Swiss Re, UBS, Unilever, Zurich.

Selected other clients: Kazakhstan prime minister & cabinet, various Swiss government agencies, UNDP, US State Department, US Air Force Academy, US Military Academy West Point.

Board member: Paramount Business Jets, Keren Hayesod World Executive, International Journal of Communication Research.

Since 2001, Thomas has taught leadership at Columbia University and since 2004 at HSG (St. Gallen University). He is often featured in the media, including ABC, Bloomberg, CNN, Swiss National TV, *Fast Company* and *Financial Times*.

Thomas is the author of seven books on co-leadership, including *Communicate or Die: Getting Results Through Speaking and Listening* (SelectBooks 2003); *Culture Clash 2.0: Managing the Global High-Performance Team* (SelectBooks 2013); *Strategy-In-Action: Marrying Planning, People and Performance* (iHorizon 2014), a Readers Favorite Silver Award winner; and *The Rabbi and the CEO: The Ten Commandments for 21st Century Leaders* (SelectBooks 2008; with Aaron L. Raskin), a National Jewish Book Award finalist.

Born in Paris, Dr. Zweifel holds a Ph.D. in International Political Economy from New York University. In 1996 he realized his dream of breaking three hours in the New York City Marathon, and in 1997 was recognized as the "fastest CEO in the New York City Marathon." He lives in Zurich with his wife and two daughters.

Other Books by Thomas D. Zweifel

Communicate or Die: Getting Results Through Speaking and Listening (SelectBooks)

> "Everybody should read this book. You can substitute one evening of entertainment and make a difference in your life and work for years to come."
> **—Ali Velshi, Senior Economic and Business Correspondent, NBC**

Culture Clash 2.0: Managing the Global High-Performance Team (SelectBooks)

> "I just wish *Culture Clash* had been available at the start of my personal globalisation, it would have saved me a lot of time and pain. I would recommend this book as essential reading for any international manager."
> **—Dr. Martin Cross, CEO, Novartis-Australia**

Democratic Deficit? Institutions and Regulation in the European Union, Switzerland and the United States (Rowman Littlefield)

> "Thomas Zweifel's pathbreaking book delivers a compelling empirical analysis of transparency and accountability in the European Union. A must-read."
> **—Andrew Moravcsik, Professor, Princeton University and *Newsweek***

International Organizations and Democracy: Accountability, Politics and Power (Lynne Rienner Publishers)

> "Zweifel's accessible book sets the stage for an informed debate on the place of 'We, The People' in global governance."
> **—Shepard Forman, Center on International Cooperation, New York University**

Strategy-In-Action: Marrying People, Planning and Performance (iHorizon; with Edward J. Borey) Silver Award, Business & Finance, Readers' Favorite

> "The only strategy book that gives a truly holistic view of strategy. It integrates strategy alignment, highly pragmatic execution and performance, and the human element in one seamless process."
> **—Dr. Frank Waltmann, Head of Learning, Novartis**

The Rabbi and the CEO: The Ten Commandments for 21st Century Leaders (SelectBooks; with Aaron L. Raskin) Finalist, National Jewish Book Award

> "The leadership wisdom contained here is timeless, powerful and actionable--just what you'd expect when you combine a Rabbi and a CEO!"
> **—Scott A. Snook, Professor of Organizational Behavior, Harvard Business School**

Forthcoming: The *iCoach®* Series

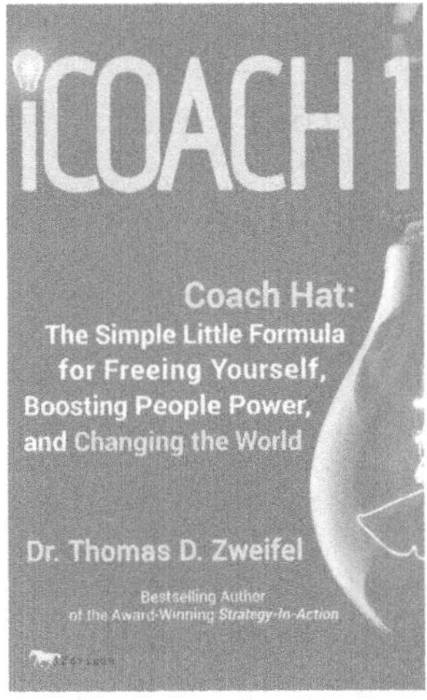

iCoach® is not just a book series. It's a 7-Step System, designed and refined over more than three decades of coaching CEOs and other leaders of all stripes to meet strategic imperatives. Even if you stay in your current job—and especially if you are the CEO—*iCoach®* gives you access to being a powerful and successful (and if you wish, financially independent) coach. *iCoach®* is your roadmap to real power—by unleashing people.

That's a mouthful. And it's a big claim. But consider this: We know how to fly a robot to Mars, but we know next to nothing about how to empower human beings—how to ignite their power and productivity. If working with other people is a mystery to you (or simply a pain in the neck), then *iCoach®* is the solution.

Is your team too dependent on you? Are you caught in micro-management or saving the day? Is there a leadership gap—or your bench strength insufficient? Are your team members not accountable, reliable, entrepreneurial or proactive enough? Do you feel at times you won't be able to stem it all, you're ready to throw in the towel or might just burn out?

Harvard Business School teaches that you can manage up to five direct reports effectively. With coaching, you don't have that constraint. *iCoach®* gives you the secret formula for leveraging yourself, making the maximum impact and growing your business when you're not around.

Thomas D. Zweifel learned coaching in the 1980s, when the profession barely existed outside of sports. He has poured his three-decade-plus experience—as a senior manager and CEO, as an entrepreneur who built a successful business named a "Fast Company" by *Fast Company* magazine, as a sought-after strategy & performance expert and CEO coach—into this series of path-breaking books. This is a Coach-in-a-Book. It's a paint-by-the-numbers, step-by-step, foolproof system. (In a word, call it Swiss.) The methodology is based on both timeless principles of leadership and the latest discoveries in brain-, neuro- and cognitive science, psycholinguistics and behavioral economics.

Dr. Zweifel has used the system himself, and still does. It helped him secure his financial freedom. He works smarter and accomplishes more, with more people, than ever. For his clients this system worked brilliantly. One top-tier energy company produced $74 million in additional revenues from innovative products that were not on the market when they started. A Swiss global bank saved $200 million. In the aggregate, Dr. Zweifel's clients have produced over $9 billion in additional revenues—while boosting innovation, aligning on new strategic frontiers and building cultures of communication and coaching.

The *iCoach*® methodology provides the kind of power Thomas believes in: power not *over* people, but power *through* people, defined as the speed from vision to achievement, from idea to realization. It's the kind of power all too often missing in companies. And it's essential to a bright future for all of us.

ThomasZweifel.com Processes

If you are interested in applying The Global Leader Pyramid® to your organization, connect to www.ThomasZweifel.com for leadership processes, coaching and workshops that help leaders open strategic frontiers, meet business imperatives and/or cause performance breakthroughs.

Strategy-In-Action: a 7-step process. Confidential and anonymous pre-interviews gather perspectives of all key stakeholders and lead to a shared understanding; a 2-day workshop aligns the management team around a bold business challenge and an elegant vision/strategy framework; and low-risk 100-Day pilots pull the future to the present, yield quick wins and provide feedback to the strategy.

Leadership-In-Action: a 2-day workshop provides leadership tools that last; systematically develops your high-potential leaders and fills their leadership gaps; and challenges their leadership in the action of meeting breakthrough goals through 100-Day leadership projects.

Coaching-In-Action: a 6-month process tailored to executives fosters breakthroughs in their leadership ability in the action of meeting a business and/or leadership challenge.

Communicate or Die: a 2-day workshop gives leaders tools for effective speaking *and* masterful listening in teams and/or organizations.

Culture Clash: a 2-day workshop prepares leaders to avoid costly mistakes when working with or in other cultures (e.g. in virtual teams and/or outsourcing), and get the job done while respecting local values and customs.

Notes

---

[1] "Citizenship in a Republic," Speech at the Sorbonne, Paris, April 23, 1910.

[2] More about leading through language in *Communicate or Die: Getting Results Through Speaking and Listening*. New York: SelectBooks.

[3] I also recommend using the Leonardo 3.4.5 self-assessment tool available at http://www.leonardo345.com/index.htm.

[4] Interview, *MarketWatch*, September 27, 2006.

[5] Richard Rapaport, "To Build a Winning Team," *Harvard Business Review* Reprint #93108.

[6] Paul, Richard and Linda Elder. 2007. "The Miniature Guide to Critical Thinking: Concepts and Tools," The Foundation for Critical Thinking. 9. See www.criticalthinking.org

[7] More about ethical leadership in *The Rabbi and the CEO: The Ten Commandments for 21st Century Leaders*. New York: SelectBooks.

[8] More about cross-cultural management in *Culture Clash 2.0: Managing the Global High-Performance Team*. New York: SelectBooks.

[9] H.W. Brands. 1999. *Masters of Enterprise*. New York: Free Press. 296.

[10] Francisco R. Sagasti, "National Development Planning in Turbulent Times: New Approaches and Criteria for Institutional Design," *World Development*, vol.16, no.4, 1988. 438.

[11] See Thomas D. Zweifel and Edward J. Borey, *Strategy-In-Action: Marrying Planning, People and Performance*. New York: iHorizon 2014.

[12] *Fortune*, June 21, 1999, 69-82.

[13] David Kearns and David Nadler. 1992. *Profits in the Dark*. New York: Harper Business Books. 249-250.

[14] *Fortune*, 21 June 1999. 70.

[15] Allan L. Scherr. 1989. "Managing for Breakthroughs in Productivity," *Human Resource Management* 28:3, Fall. 403-424.

[16] P.Ranganath Nayak and John M. Ketteringham. 1986. *Breakthroughs!* New York: Rawson Associates. 347.

[17] Rosa Parks, interview, http://teacher.scholastic.com/rosa/arrested.htm

[18] H.W. Brands. *Masters of Enterprise: Giants of American Business from John Jacob Astor and J.P. Morgan to Bill Gates and Oprah Winfrey*. New York: The Free Press, 1999.

[19] The Hunger Project, unpublished manuscript, 1985.
[20] *New York Times* magazine, November 29, 1998.
[21] Genesis, 1:3-5.
[22] *The Economist*, op.cit., p. 26.

Made in the USA
Monee, IL
06 November 2020

46887520R10144